GameChangers

*The Men and Women
Who Changed Sports
In Our Lifetime*

By Dave Kocak

Untiliwin Press
Buffalo, New York

Dedication

For Joanne

Table of Contents

Preface 9

Introduction 10

Rule Breakers and Rule Makers 13

Wilt Chamberlain...15

Kareem Abdul-Jabbar 17

Olga Korbut...18

Torvill and Dean..19

Money, Money, Money...21

Mark McCormack and Arnold Palmer..................... 23

Marvin Miller and Curt Flood 27

Bill Rasmussen 31

Innovators...35

Bill Russell 37

Bobby Orr..39

Maury Wills...41

Jimmy Arias...46

Dick Fosbury...49

Football Innovators 54

John Mackey..53

Pete Gogolak 54

Deion Sanders 56

Lawrence Taylor 57

Trailblazers Part I: The Foreigners........................59

Borje Salming.. 63

Marciulonis and Sabonis..64

Hideo Nomo 65

Chan Ho Park 66

Se Ri Pak 67

Trailblazers Part II: The Americans 69

Moses Malone 69

Diane Crump..71

Julie Krone...72

Rosie Napravnik..73

Table of Contents (cont)

Science and Technology **75**
  Howard Head 77
  Dr. Frank Jobe And Tommy John.............................. 81
  Victor Conte 83
  Dr. Bennett Omalu... 87
  Bill James 90

More Basketball **95**
  Cousy and the boys... 96
  Spud Webb 101

More Tennis **103**
  Billie Jean King... 105
  Chris Evert.. 107
  Martina Navratilova.. 109
  Nick Bolletieri 111

Sports and Society **115**
  James Harris, First Black Quarterback 117
  Muhammad Ali 122
  Coming Out... 124
  Jason Collins 127
  Michael Sam.. 128
  Patsy Mink and Edith Green 130

Lance Armstrong... **133**

Outliers **135**

Modern Sports: Pro and Con... **137**

Epilogue... **139**

Acknowledgements... **141**

Preface

I love reading and I love books. I have a wide range of interests; sports, history, sports history, social science, economics, language and politics. These are all popular subjects with new books galore appearing every month.

With all these new titles, combined with all the current books I haven't gotten to, the problem is, and always will be, a lack of reading time. One of the ways I maximize my reading time is to avoid large books with small print that tell me in great detail everything there is to know about a subject.

The ancient history book that carefully differentiates the writings of Pliny from Pliny the Elder is not making good use of my time. The sports biography that details every "magical" season is likewise unlikely to keep me involved.

I don't have time for such a thorough explanation of anything. If you feel the same way, you may have gotten just the right book. My research is accurate but not overwhelming. I have attempted to give an overview of the changes in sports in the last 50 years, nothing more. My opinions, while brilliant and insightful, are just that, opinions. They may start more conversations than they resolve.

I hope you find this book informative, enjoyable and thought provoking. If not, at least you didn't spend too much time getting through it.

Introduction

When the thought came to me to write about how sports had changed, I wasn't sure what form it would take. It has become a book about changes in sports in my lifetime (1951-present) and from an American perspective. If you want to know how European soccer changed in the 1960s, you won't find it here. I was lucky to be able to write anything about ice hockey in the NHL, let alone anything about sports in the rest of the world.

For the most part, I have concentrated on professional sports or Olympic sports rather than college or amateurs. Of course there is an exception to this.

By 1951, most sports had been around for a while and changing them in any meaningful way was not easy. Baseball pitchers had been throwing curveballs (not the optical illusion they originally thought it was) for a long time and homeruns were an integral part of the sport. Babe Ruth was a game changer, but his most profound impact on baseball occurred in the 1920s. Football has been throwing the forward pass for a long time and the jump shot has been the preferred method of shooting in basketball since anyone alive can remember. In fact, the older and more mature the sport, the harder it was to find a real game changer.

Very few sports have had major changes in technique in this time period, although there are a couple of exceptions. Often these exceptions are technology related; many of these changes took place far from the playing field.

Tennis is unique in the sense that although it's been around since the 1880s, professional tennis, and the money associated with professional sports, only appeared in 1968. Some of the Olympic sports also advanced later when riches could be had for the price of a gold medal. Often the game changers were those who led a new group of participants into the sport.

Surprisingly, many of the game changers included in this book never played the sports they changed, at least they never played them at a very high level.

I hope you will find some other surprises too.

I apologize in advance for omitting someone you feel changed your favorite sport. This book in no way pretends to be the ultimate source for all sports and the changes that occurred and why. It is the product of my personal observations and personal research and is bound to have missed at least a few "game changers."

Rule Makers
and Rule Breakers

Rule Makers and Rule Breakers

"You no playa da game, you no makea da rules!"

Italian woman's English response to
Pope John Paul's continued ban on birth control.

Sports must have rules and rules are made by men and women. Some sports rarely change their rules. Baseball, for instance, has had almost no rule changes for over a hundred years. With the exception of the designated hitter rule (in the American League) and the occasional change of the height of the pitcher's mound or the size of the strike zone, nothing has changed since the turn of the last century. On the other hand, football, has proven more adaptable. It has a rules committee that introduces changes every season, usually minor, but not always. In 2015 they discussed eliminating the extra point after touchdowns, but settled on moving it back 20 yards so as not to be automatic. They are more than willing to make changes whenever the offensive/defensive balance of the game seems threatened. The NBA added the three-point shot in the 1979-80 season, momentous, but not much since. Changes mostly address how physical they will let the players be.

Olympic sports haven't changed a whole lot, particularly with the sclerotic leadership it has had for almost its entire history. The acknowledged founder, Baron de Coupertin, was staunchly against women competitors. Later, Avery Brundage and his emphasis on amateurism stripped the great Jim Thorpe of his Olympic medals based on his appearance in semi-pro baseball games. And, Juan Antonio Samaranch who, while finally allowing professional athletes to participate, negating the Communist Bloc countries advantage with their "amateur" athletes, was also in charge when bribing of Olympic officials became the norm.

The biggest changes in Olympic sports were made by women, who were at first thought to be too frail to compete in stamina and strength events. The first women's gymnastics events in 1928 included rope climbing of all things. Through the years women's events became more demanding, but the first women's marathon had to wait until 1984. Now, back to the rules:

Wilt Chamberlain

"Everyone roots for David. No one cheers for Goliath."
Wilt Chamberlain

Wilt Chamberlain, the first 7' 1" goliath to enter the NBA forced several rule changes before and during his playing days. First and foremost they widened the three second lane, forcing Wilt to set up further from the basket. They eliminated the running start and dunk for a free throw which only Chamberlain could accomplish. This is particularly odd as there are no references to him shooting them that way. The league also disallowed inbounding the ball by throwing it over the basket, which many feared would be an automatic two points if Wilt could catch it there. Later, they put in a rule regarding offensive goaltending, preventing Wilt from guiding his teammates' shots to the basket.

Of course, even from the wider lane, Wilt was still able to get to the basket. The "no offensive goaltending" rule didn't keep him from being the best offensive rebounder in the league. It was only his foul shooting which may have suffered from the rule change. Wilt was never a good free throw shooter and ended his career with a .511 free throw percentage.

Though he prompted many rule changes to contain his talents, he remains the greatest single force in the history of basketball, averaging as many as 50 points in a season.

Winner of two NBA championships, he was often defeated by his long time competitor Bill Russell and the Boston Celtics. Whenever someone would suggest to Russell that he had outplayed Chamberlain, Russell was quick to point out that when Chamberlain set the single game rebounding record of 55, Russell was his opponent.

Yes, he was ahead of his time and the first athletic seven-footer. Had he grown up in a different era, he would probably have dominated that era as well.

In later life, when asked who was greater, Michael Jordan or himself, Chamberlain summarized his argument this way. "When Michael played, they changed the rules to make it easier for him. When I played, they changed the rules to make it harder for me." It can be a persuasive argument.

Kareem Abdul-Jabbar

"I can do something else besides stuff a ball through a hoop."
My biggest resource is my mind.

Kareem Abdul-Jabbar

In 1966 the unquestioned greatest high school basketball player in all the land was Lew Alcindor, of Power Memorial High School in New York City, 7' 1" tall and a dunking machine. While on his way to UCLA, a funny thing happened. The college basketball fathers at the NCAA banned dunking! They banned it from the games and even from the warmup. I guess they were afraid the fans might show up for the pregame and leave before the game. I can imagine a highlight reel of pregame dunks that the fans knew they would not see during the game. If ever there was a rule made by old white guys trying to stop a black man, this has to be it, at least as far as sports are concerned. It didn't stop him, of course. It just made the game less exciting. Alcindor won three NCAA titles, averaged over twenty-five points a game while losing only two games in his career. After college he became a Muslim, changed his name to Kareem Abdul-Jabbar, and scared those old white guys even more. Most high schools played by NCAA rules which meant that they weren't allowed to dunk either. Consequently, as a high school player of that era, I was unfairly prevented from passing a ball to someone who could dunk.

The no-dunking rule wasn't changed until 1976, I guess to make sure that he wasn't coming back to college and that no one could accuse them of creating the rule just for him.

Kareem went on to become the NBA's career all-time leading scorer.

Olga Korbut

"If there had not been such a thing as gymnastics, I would have had to invent it because I feel at one with the sport."
Olga Korbut

Move ahead to 1972 and Munich, West Germany. Women's gymnastics – uneven bars. 17 year old Russian Olga Korbut begins her routine with some nice moves, but nothing out of the ordinary. Then she stands atop the high bar, does a backward 360 degree somersault and returns to the bar. Suddenly women's gymnastics is changed forever. We have gone from 1928 rope climbing to 1972 flying. A 9.8 score from the judges is roundly booed. Every 18 year old gymnast thinking about the 1976 Olympics might as well pick up her slippers and go home. Artistry is dead. Superhuman athleticism is in, and that can only be performed by pre-pubescent females. Women need not apply. The judges, probably as stunned as everyone else, chose not to penalize or ban what came to be known as the "Korbut Flip." Had they done so, women's gymnastics might have stayed where it was and we wouldn't have been treated to the sensational Nadia Comaneci and her perfect scores four years later in Montreal. Her performance, and the roar of approval that it caused, cemented the pre-eminence of athleticism over style; flips and leaps over grace.

Ludmilla Tourischeva won the 1972 All-around Gymnastics title at the age of 20, after beginning gymnastics at the age of 13. Today's gymnasts peak at 16 and most are retired at 20.

Olga, though injured, earned a team gold and an individual silver medal in the 1976 Olympics.

In 1991 she emigrated to the United States and lives in Scottsdale, Arizona where she has taught gymnastics for many years.

Competition being what it is, and Olympic Gold being the intoxicant that it is, it was inevitable that new moves, more difficult and dangerous than before would creep into the routines. Eventually, some moves were deemed too dangerous for competition and had to be banned, including the Korbut Flip. Otherwise, we might see some horrific injuries in our living rooms, instead of on the practice floor where they belong.

Torvill and Dean

"An art form requires genius. People of genius are always troublemakers, meaning they start from scratch, demolish accepted norms, and rebuild a new world."
Henri Langlois

Let's go forward to Sarajevo, 1984 Winter Olympics. The sport is ice dancing. Ice dancing? Is that even a sport? Nothing is more boring than ice dancing. No Peggy Flemings or Dorothy Hamills here. This is a sport dominated for years by tuxedoed Russian men with elegant, though stark Russian women doing dance steps no one has done for years to the music of dead Russian composers. Look, they're doing the foxtrot or maybe a waltz or tango. Wake me when the killing starts!

No, wait. It's different now. Really! There's an English couple: Jayne Torvill and Christopher Dean. Jayne was a former British Junior Pairs Champion and Christopher was a former Junior Ice Dance winner. Their first Olympics was in Lake Placid, NY where they finished fifth. Everything about them is different. Their costumes are brilliant, their choreography is out of this world and their skating and teamwork are remarkable. They are so good that American television is going to feature them even though they aren't American and no one cares about ice dancing.

They dance to Ravel's Bolero. From beginning to end they are mesmerizing. No triple toe-loops or double salchows, just two skaters in perfect harmony with the music and with each other in a dance that has to be experienced to be believed and can't be explained. Watch it yourself on YouTube.

At the end, commentator and former Olympic skating champ Peggy Fleming exclaims that we were so lucky to be able to see this and former champ Dick Button says they broke all the rules and none of it matters. The judges agree. 5.9 and 6.0 scores across the board for technical merit, and a perfect run of 6.0s for artistic merit. Highest scores ever. A Gold Medal and international acclaim follow and riches from the Ice Capades or their equivalent.

In 1994, in Lilliehammer, Norway a comeback is attempted. Not so fast you English upstarts. The trends you have started have gotten out of control. Free dance routines have turned into mini-operas filled with gorgeous costumes and drama. Yes, I said drama! The old white people who control the sport don't like drama, and don't like where this has been going. They cringe every time they hear Bolero, no matter what the context.

Torvill and Dean are again in a position to win a gold medal and again they perform exquisitely, having lost none of their skill nor their creativity. They dance to an upbeat version of "Let's face the Music and Dance" and as they face the music and the judges they get slapped down into a bronze medal. The judges are tired of this s---, and they make the rules and things are going to change. Of course, nobody cares about ice dancing ever again. Yes, the Americans and Canadians are now the countries to beat, but nobody really cares.

Ultimately, it's the rule makers who rule the sport. Fortunately, the profit motive, meaning how many eyeballs will watch it on television, usually rules the day, but not always.

Money,
Money, Money

Money, Money, Money

Where did all this money come from? In the 1950s baseball, football and basketball players, by necessity, all had off-season jobs. Tennis players were paid under the table, if at all. American golfers didn't play the British Open because the prize money didn't even cover expenses. Olympic athletes couldn't train properly because they were either college students or working full-time jobs. What happened?

Here's what happened...

Arnold Palmer and
Mark McCormack

"You don't have to reinvent the wheel. Just attach it to a different wagon."
Mark McCormack

My first football card, way back in 1961, was of Eddie LeBaron. The back of the card read simply "Eddie Lebaron, the first quarterback of the Dallas Cowboys, at 5' 9" is the shortest quarterback in the NFL. In the off-season he sells insurance."

Sells insurance? I guess you gotta make ends meet somehow. And that was the sports world that Mark McCormack entered in 1959.

In 1959 athletes worked in off-season jobs to support their families. In 1959 their outside endorsements consisted of a few dollars from TOPPS sports cards or the use of a car from a car dealership for a commercial or the occasional $50 from a Little League banquet speaking engagement. If you were lucky, they put your name on some equipment and kicked you a very small percentage for the privilege.

The very best players always did well, but the average player had to hustle to make ends meet.

Mark McCormack, a Yale Law school graduate practicing in Cleveland, Ohio didn't much care for the idea of handling wills and mortgages for the rest of his days and thought he could make some money for pro golfers by setting them up with exhibitions during the week before the weekend tournament. He signed Arnold Palmer, winner of the 1958 Masters, Gene Littler, Julius Boros and a handful of others.

It was not as easy as it looked and ultimately failed, but what finally emerged from the effort was an agreement for McCormack to represent Arnold Palmer exclusively.

Athletes almost never had representation. They almost never made enough to warrant giving someone 10% for handling their endorsements. Babe Ruth and Lou Gehrig were promoted and represented by Christy Walsh, baseball's first agent, who made a series of movies and exhibition games with them, but most players represented themselves. No one ever had an agent negotiate a contract for them.

Arnold Palmer had his wife doing most of the things an agent would take care of. There were no lawyers around to review contracts or negotiate deals. It was not a sophisticated operation.

In 1957 Palmer won $29,000 on the PGA Tour. In 1958 he won his first Masters title and $44,000 in prize money. In 1959, $35,000. Like all athletes, golfers have a limited window of opportunity to make their fortune. Despite his success on the course, this was not the kind of cash one could retire on when his golfing days were over, not even in 1960 dollars.

McCormack thought that athletes were very marketable commodities. After all, didn't everyone want to be around baseball, football or golf stars?

When Palmer committed to McCormack it seemed like a perfect opportunity to show all athletes how underpaid and exploited they were.

For instance, Palmer, in 1961 the biggest name in golf and one of America's biggest sports stars, was going to make about $21,000 on $1,250,000 in sales of Wilson's Arnold Palmer Signature golf clubs. It was a great deal for Wilson, and one that came with a three year extension if Wilson wanted it, and they did.

McCormack attempted to renegotiate the deal. Palmer wasn't even aware of the three year extension option they had quietly snuck into the contract. If the deal wasn't renegotiated Palmer would certainly leave Wilson in 1964 after the contract expired. Wouldn't you want to keep Arnold Palmer, the most charismatic golfer to come along in ages, representing your product? Wilson took the short view, the quick money, and the decades long regret.

McCormack convinced Palmer that "Arnold Palmer" was more than a name, it was a brand. And brands mean something. Think of "Cadillac," "Chanel," "Armani."

Once free of the Wilson contract, McCormack and Palmer turned the "Arnold Palmer" brand into one of sports' most successful businesses. It didn't hurt that Palmer had won several Majors, some with exciting last round charges, and by 1964 was the most popular golfer and one of the most popular athletes in the country. McCormack, beginning with the marketing success of Arnold Palmer, created an agency (IMG) that now represents over a thousand athletes, Wimbledon Tennis, and the IMG sports training complex in Florida.

In 1990, *The Sporting News* named him the most powerful man in sports. Mark McCormack passed away in 2003 from a heart attack. Upon his death, International Management Group (IMG) was worth $1.6 billion. Posthumously, he was inducted into the "World Golf Hall of Fame" and the "International Tennis Hall of Fame." No athlete is likely to ever achieve that honor.

By his death in 2016, Palmer owned Bay Hill Golf Club in Orlando, Florida, a golf course construction business, an airplane business and 10% of International Management Group (IMG).

Thanks to McCormack and game changers like Marvin Miller, pro athletes are not just envied for their on-field prowess, but now for their paychecks as well.

Athletes no longer negotiate their own contracts or seek out their own endorsement deals; sports agents represent them now. 10% of an athlete's earnings is no longer an insignificant sum of money. Top athletes make millions from their sport and many times that from outside endorsement deals. Whether it's equipment, soft drinks, autos, shoes or jewelry, the best athletes now earn in the hundreds of millions of dollars over a career. Michael Jordan, Lebron James and Tiger Woods are each worth more than $1 Billion.

Marvin Miller and Curt Flood

*"To the estimable Marvin Miller - Whose contributions to baseball
continue to be ignored by those blinded by their own ignorance.
With respect, regret and apologies."*

Former Baseball Commissioner Fay Vincent's dedication to his book
"We would have played for Nothing"

1950s Dodger pitcher Carl Erskine tells the story of walking into General Manager Branch Rickey's office to negotiate his next year's contract. He'd had a good year and was hoping for a $2,500 raise. Mr. Rickey invited him to sit down and began by saying "Carl, you had a pretty good year last year. We've decided to invite you back!"

And that was it. End of negotiation. Back in those days, Major League Baseball had an anti-trust exemption and the reserve clause, which stated that a player could play only for the team he had played for the previous season or be forced to retire. Normal labor law did not apply. All the negotiating leverage belonged to the baseball owners.

Marvin Miller was a former U.S. government economist and an economist and negotiator for the United Steel Workers. In 1966 he became the Executive Director of the Major League Baseball Players Association (MLBPA). The Players Association at that time had no budget and no successes to show for their efforts. He convinced 500 competitive individuals that solidarity and collective bargaining were the keys to their success. He successfully negotiated with the TOPPS card company over compensation for player pictures to be used on baseball cards. That gave him an operating budget. He then bargained for a raise in the minimum salary from $6,000 to $10,000. That was just the beginning.

Curt Flood grew up in Oakland, California and played on the same baseball team with future major leaguers Frank Robinson and Vada Pinson. Signed by the Cincinnati Reds in 1956, he spent a couple of seasons in the South in the minor leagues.

His horrible treatment as a black man in the Jim Crow South made a lasting impression on Flood. He would never be treated as a second class citizen again.

After being traded to St. Louis, he flourished, earning four All-Star appearances and seven consecutive Gold Gloves. He played 12 seasons for the St. Louis Cardinals before he was traded to the Philadelphia Phillies in 1969. While in St. Louis he had begun a successful portrait studio which he did not want to abandon in a move to Philadelphia. He refused to go to Philadelphia and sent a letter to Commissioner Bowie Kuhn informing him of his decision.

"After twelve years in the major leagues, I do not feel I am a piece of property to be bought and sold irrespective of my wishes. I believe that any system which produces that result violates my basic rights as a citizen and is inconsistent with the laws of the United States and of the several States."

Curt Flood

At $90,000 a year, Flood did not get much sympathy from the general public, where the average fan made less than 1/5 of that. Flood himself acknowledged this by referring to himself as "A well-paid slave."

Marvin Miller convinced the Major League Players' union to back Flood's lawsuit against Major League Baseball's "reserve clause," which effectively bound a player to one team for his entire career, or to be traded at the team's discretion.

In 1970 the players won the right to independent arbitration of grievances rather than being judged by the Commissioner of Baseball who worked for the owners. The walls around the owners' labor model were beginning to crumble.

Professional football, basketball and hockey took a keen interest in Flood's case and all the players' associations supported him.

Flood's case went all the way to the Supreme Court and in 1972 the court ruled in favor of Major League Baseball. Despite the loss, Flood felt vindicated. He was deeply hurt by the fact that no players supported him during his lawsuit, not even Vada Pinson or Frank Robinson, who may have stayed away from the controversy as he wanted to become baseball's first black manager.

The case took a severe toll on Flood's personal and professional life. He was threatened by fans who thought he was trying to kill baseball. He sat out the 1970 season. Out of shape and his skills diminished by alcoholism, he played only 13 games for the Washington Senators in 1971 before retiring.

Even though Flood lost, he was the first to chip away at the reserve clause. Others would follow.

After a contract dispute between owner Charlie Finley of the Oakland A's and pitcher Jim "Catfish" Hunter went to arbitration, Hunter became a free agent when it was determined that Finley had not lived up to his part of the contract.

Hunter, the premier pitcher in baseball, showed other players what was possible as a free agent when he signed a contract with the New York Yankees for $3.5 million with a $1 million signing bonus.

Mark McCormack's long ago understanding of how grossly underpaid athletes were was finally proven true.

In 1975, in a case brought by Baltimore Orioles' pitchers Andy Messersmith and Dave McNally, an arbitrator ruled that by playing out the options on their contracts they were now free agents, and the "reserve clause" was officially dead.

Guess what? Baseball survived and even thrived. Players' salaries took off into the astronomical heights that we see today. Attendance has never been stronger.

It was agreed that players could become free agents after six years in the major leagues. Salaries increased during Miller's time as director from $19,000 on average, to $326,000.

All this was not achieved without some friction. There were strikes in 1972, 1980 and 1981. The players were locked out in 1973 and 1976. The strike of 1994-95 was the first to prevent the World Series.

The MLBPA became the first of pro sports players' associations to achieve free agent status and remains the strongest of the sports unions. MLB is the only league without a salary cap.

Curt Flood died in 1997, a victim of throat cancer. He was a proud man who stuck to his principles and was proved right in the end.

Marvin Miller is often said to be, along with Babe Ruth and Jackie Robinson, one of the three most influential people in the history of baseball. His induction into the Baseball Hall of Fame occurred in, no, wait, he never got into the Hall of Fame! The committee selecting executives for the Hall was changed from a players committee to one with only two of twelve members being players. The last vote had Miller receiving only 4 of 12 votes. The owners have a long memory.

Marvin Miller died in 2012 at the age of 95.

Bill Rasmussen

"We believe that the appetite for sports in this country is insatiable."
Bill Rasmussen

ESPN, the Entertainment and Sports Network was conceived in 1978 by Bill Rasmussen. Bill Rasmussen worked for several New England TV stations before he became the communications director for the World Hockey Association's Hartford Whalers. After the 1977-78 season, the Whalers, hemorrhaging money, fired Bill Rasmussen. Bill conceived of a Sports Network and decided to name it The Entertainment and Sports Programming Network or ESPN. Rasmussen sold 85% of his fledgling network to Getty Oil to buy land in Bristol, Connecticut for the satellite broadcast center. Launched in September 1979 with the first edition of SportsCenter, its iconic and signature program, ESPN became the first 24-hour sports programming network.

Begun with the help of money from Anheuser-Busch, the "official beer of ESPN," it was broadcast to 1.4 million cable subscribers. Now it is broadcast to 94 million homes or over 80% of homes with a television set. Rasmussen was quickly cut out of the operating picture and was named "Chairman."

Its thirst for programming and limited budget led to game replays and quirky sports like the ever-popular Australian Rules Football, a game Americans had no understanding of, but found oddly entertaining.

Initially, ESPN was on the fringes of big time sports programming, broadcasting the early rounds of the NCAA basketball tournament or the NFL Draft but yielding to the major networks for the actual premier events.

The viewership for events like the early rounds of tennis' U.S. Open or golf's Masters was surprisingly high. Nobody quite knew how truly insatiable America's sports junkies were.

Purchased in 1984 by ABC, ESPN was able to compete for broadcast rights to major events. A Supreme Court ruling allowed for multiple college football games to be broadcast to a region in the same weekend, allowing for NCAA football and basketball to fill up the channel from noon EST to midnight PCT. In 1987 ESPN began broadcasting Sunday Night NFL Football. SNF remained its highest rated show until NBC won the rights in 2009.

Twenty-four hours a day of sports programming was not enough, so ABC launched ESPN2 in 1993, a year after beginning ESPN radio.

In 1996 The Walt Disney Company bought ESPN and it is now Disney's largest revenue source.

ESPN is thoroughly embedded in our culture. Every athlete's dream is to appear in the Top Ten Highlights on SportsCenter. Daytime is filled with sports talk television and radio. No controversy is so small or large that it can't be amplified by 24-hour sports talk coverage.

Botched plays, missed opportunities and controversial decisions live on and on. A video of an athlete striking his girlfriend in an elevator or a coach making a racial, sexist or homophobic remark near a microphone leads to replays ad nauseum and ruined careers.

ESPN also does some quality journalism with its "E-60" investigative news magazine and its weekly show "Outside the Lines"; its "30 for 30" documentaries often deal with important subjects in depth.

Now there is ESPN News and ESPN Desportes for Spanish speakers.

Major events are now more likely to appear on ESPN than the major networks, particularly overseas events that may not be live in primetime. Events like the World Cup or Wimbledon are almost exclusively on ESPN, increasingly big U.S. events like NCAA basketball and football playoffs and NFL and NBA playoffs appear on the network.

The programming needs of all these channels often leads to extremes. As an example, there are now 40 FBS Bowl games, all broadcast on TV, most on ESPN. In 1978 there were only 12. My current favorite is the "Famous Idaho Potato Bowl" in Boise, Idaho in December. Once a reward for an outstanding season, a bowl appearance is now available to any team that can field 22 players and has a good excuse for why they don't have a winning record. Sometimes the excuse doesn't even have to be good.

Revenue from TV is supposed to pay for bowl committee and school expenses because the empty stadium crowds certainly can't. Oftentimes it does not. You now have a situation where many schools turn down bowl invitations.

Still, the programming needs continue. The network name seems to be missing a "T", as in ESPTN, the "Entertainment and Sports Talk Network." Shows like ESPN's "For the Record," ESPN's "Off the Record," and ESPN's "Broken Record" redundantly fill up the programming day.

Battles over subscriber rates have led to a current loss of subscribers, but the behemoth that is ESPN will neither go away nor lose its influence any time soon. Bill Rasmussen had it right. The American desire for sports programming is insatiable. I just don't know for how long!

Innovators

Innovators

There's a way to do it better – find it!
Thomas Edison

As the introduction suggested, innovation on the field in modern sports is not common but it happens from time to time. The athletes in this section brought some new element to their sport or changed something basic. Some changed their sport through individual strengths and some through individual weakness that had to be overcome. All required new thinking and hard work and overcoming the naysayers who couldn't see the potential for improvements in the change.

Bill Russell

"Basketball is like war in that offensive weapons are developed first, and it always takes a while for the defense to catch up."
Red Auerbach

In 1957 The NBA had been in existence for 11 years. They introduced the 24 second shot clock only in the 1954-55 season. Before that, some games were dreadfully boring with the team ahead often holding the ball for the entire quarter. Teams were in small cities like Syracuse, New York and Fort Wayne, Indiana. The league was almost entirely white.

This was the NBA Bill Russell joined in the fall of 1957. Red Auerbach desperately wanted Russell on the Boston Celtics. Auerbach knew better than anyone else in the league his true value, and gave up two star players and a draft pick to get him.

Bill Russell was a 6' 9" black man from Oakland, California. He played his college basketball at the University of San Francisco where they were a two-time NCAA Champion and owner of a 56-game winning streak. When west coast sportswriters implored the NY Times and other prominent eastern newspapers to write about Russell and USF, the reply was often "We looked at the box score and saw that he had six points last night. What's the big deal?"

The big deal was that Russell was a defensive genius. Sound fundamental basketball defense of the day demanded that you keep your feet on the ground, maintaining good position between your opponent and the basket. Russell was jumping all over the place. Not without purpose, of course, but jumping to block shots, something he did over and over again. A proud and stubborn man, Russ continued to fight with his college coach throughout his career over the value of keeping your feet on the ground to play good defense. Amazingly, Russell never won that argument.

Modern shot-blocking is most impressive when the shot blocker sends the shot into the second row of the stands. Russell thought that was ridiculous. When he blocked a shot, he tried to direct it to a teammate to start a fast break in the other direction.

Bill Russell was the first player to embody the concept that good defense could be the start of your offense. An outstanding rebounder, he developed a quick outlet pass that started the Celtics on their devastating fast break.

Shot blocking was not kept as a statistic during Russell's career but rebounding was and Russell led the league in rebounding for four seasons and was second to Wilt Chamberlain after that. In an era when there were far more rebounds in a game than today, Russell averaged more than 20 rebounds a game and he and Chamberlain are the only players to record 50 rebounds in a game.

....

"The idea is not to block every shot. The idea is to make your opponent believe that you might block every shot."
Bill Russell

....

It's hard to know how many shots Russell actually blocked in a game. With no official records to back them up, the recollections of teammates and others seem fantastical, yet he is acknowledged by those who played in his era as the greatest shot blocker of all time. When Mr. Russell eventually passes away, I'm sure the number of blocks will only grow larger.

Russell was never better than the third best scorer on his team, yet he won five league Most Valuable Player Awards. He won 11 NBA Championships in 13 seasons. He won with teammates Bob Cousy and Bill Sharman in the 1950s and with Sam Jones and John Havlicek in the 1960s. He won with Red Auerbach as coach, and then as player-coach himself. The only constant was that Bill Russell was the center for all those teams. He also won two high school state championships, two

NCAA championships and an Olympic Gold Medal in 1956.

When anyone discusses the greatest winner in sports, Bill Russell is at the top of the list.

When anyone discusses the greatest defender and shot-blocker, there is no list. Only Bill Russell.

Bobby Orr

"You don't win by being good. You win with hard work and sacrifice. Without that, talent is just potential."
Bobby Orr

Harry Howell, upon winning the Norris Trophy as the NHL's best defenseman in 1966-67 said, "I'm glad I won it now, because it's going to belong to that Orr from now on." And so it did, for the next eight seasons.

Born in Parry Sound, Ontario in 1948, Bobby Orr was quickly spotted as a future star and never failed to live up to that potential.

From his rookie year in 1966 until he retired in 1979, Bobby Orr brought offense to defense in a way no other defenseman had. No defenseman had scored twenty goals in a season in more than two decades before Orr. He did it for seven consecutive seasons, five seasons with more than 30 and 46 in 1974-75. He led the league in assists in five seasons, including 102 in 1970-71 while leading the Boston Bruins to the Stanley Cup. No other defenseman has ever done it once. He even led the league in points, twice. Only Wayne Gretzky has ever led the league in assists more often (16).

The league had never seen a defenseman like Bobby Orr before, and they haven't seen one like him since, but it is now not uncommon to see an offense minded defenseman. Dennis Potvin of the NY Islanders scored more than 20 goals eight times, scoring 30 three times. Brian

Leetch of the NY Rangers, (5 times), Ray Bourque of the Boston Bruins (7 times), Phil Housley of the Buffalo Sabres (7 times) and Paul Coffey of the Edmonton Oilers (8 times) followed in Orr's footsteps. Coffey even scored 48 goals in 1985-86, two better than Orr's best goal scoring season.

Orr's career was limited by repeated knee injuries and was effectively ended in 1975 at the age of 27, even though he didn't officially retire until three years later.

Orr is the only player to win three consecutive MVP awards. Hockey became a better and much more exciting sport because of Bobby Orr. Orr is still active as a sports agent for a number of hockey players.

Maury Wills

Baseball in the 1950s according to Bill James in the Baseball Abstract was *"the most one-dimensional, uniform, predictable version of the game ever offered to the public. By 1950 the stolen base was a rare play, a "surprise" play."*

In 1956 Luis Aparicio of the Chicago White Sox was Rookie of the Year in the American League and led the league in stolen bases with 21. 21! Willie Mays led the majors with 40 stolen bases with Aparicio tied with Junior Gilliam of the Brooklyn Dodgers for 2nd. 37 year old Pee Wee Reese was 8th in the majors with 13 stolen bases. 13???? The rest of the 1950s was more of the same, with Aparicio leading the American League and Willie Mays the National, and 18 steals putting you in the top five in either league.

The 1959 pennant winning Chicago White Sox stole 113 bases while getting caught 53 times. Aparicio stole half of those (56) while getting caught just 13 times. The rest of the team stole 57 while being caught 40 times for just a 59% success rate, and this team was called the "Go-Go Sox"! I think that was because they played in the "Go Slow" league. This was the state of baseball when Maury Wills entered in 1959. After 8 years in the minors, Wills was called up by the Los Angeles Dodgers for the 2nd half of the season. His minor league career barely revealed a glimpse of what was to come. His highest stolen base total in the minors was 25, twice with Spokane in Triple-A, but the second time was in only 48 games before he was called up to the Dodgers.

In 1960, his first full year in the majors, he led the National League in steals with 50, while being thrown out only 12 times. He led the league again in 1961 with 35 steals.

1962 promised to be a special season. The Dodgers appeared to be the best team in baseball, led by pitchers Sandy Koufax and Don Drysdale and outfielders Tommy and Willie Davis (no relation), and Maury Wills let everyone know he was out to beat Ty Cobbs' record of 96 stolen bases in a season, set in 1915.

There is something special about trying to beat a long standing record, particularly one held by a legend like Ty Cobb. Cobbs' 96 stolen base season was almost as sacred as Dimaggio's 56-game hitting streak, or Babe Ruth's 60 homerun season or 714 career homeruns. Yet, records are sometimes made to be broken.

Cobb followed up his record setting year with 68 steals in 1916, a year in which Max Carey stole 63. Only Ben Chapman in 1931 (61 steals) and George Case in 1943 (61) had broken 60, and Chapman never came close again, while Case had achieved his mark in the talent-ravaged years of WWII. So in 1962, no one but Cobb himself and Max Carey had come within 33 steals of the record that was set in 1916. To break the record, it would take better than a 60% improvement over the best base stealers of the last 45 years.

Imagine attempting to be 50% better than the best homerun hitters to beat Babe Ruth, or to achieve a 50% better batting average than the current best to beat Ted Williams mark of .406. That's what Wills proposed to do in breaking the mark of the great Ty Cobb.

Mays and Aparicio were indeed adding much-needed excitement to the game, but the assault on one of baseball's most hallowed records captured the attention of the nation.

By June 25th Wills had stolen 35 bases in only 40 attempts and it was mentioned that 60 stolen bases might be reached for the first time in almost 20 years. As Fall approached and the stolen bases piled up, Baseball Commissioner Ford Frick decreed that just as he had with Roger Maris the previous year, Wills would need to break Ty Cobb's mark of 96 stolen bases in 154 games, instead of the 162 games the Major Leagues now played. Actually, Cobb needed 156 games, as two games that year ended in a tie due to darkness.

As Maury was racking up the stolen bases, he had also developed a nasty hematoma (a swelling of clotted blood within the tissues) on his right thigh from his hip to his knee. He only slid on his right side, with his left leg extended to the far side of the base, so his right leg took all the abuse. It took at least 30 minutes daily in the trainer's room to get him ready to play.

In game #156 Wills stole bases 96 and 97 breaking Cobb's record and finishing the season with 104 steals while being caught only 13 times. Major League Baseball still required the dreaded asterisk, stating that since Wills did not break the record in 154 games, there were now two stolen base records. In 1974 Lou Brock would break both, getting his 97th steal before game 154 and stealing a total of 118.

Unfortunately for Wills and the Dodgers, future Hall of Fame pitcher Sandy Koufax missed the last two months of the season with an injury and the season ended with the San Francisco Giants tied with the Dodgers for first place in the National League. A three game playoff was won by the Giants and off to the World Series they went, losing to the New York Yankees in six games.

So what happened to Major League Baseball after 1962? Here's a chart of league base-stealing stats from the early 1950s to the current day. Major League Stealing Stats

Year	Stolen Bases (SB)	Caught Stealing (CS)	SB%
2015	2505	1064	70%
2005	2565	1069	71%
1995	2933	1257	70%
1985	3097	1431	68%
1975	2524	1369	65%
1965	1449	784	65%
1964	1176	719	62%
1963	1236	763	62%
1962	1348	701	66%
1960	923	547	63%
1958	741	516	59%
1952	771	628	55%

Success rates for steals in the 1950s were abysmal. Modern day analytics value a stolen base as two-tenths (.2) of a run, while getting caught is a negative thirty- five hundredths of a run (-.35). With success rates in the American League never greater than 58% and the National exceeding 60% only later in the decade, you may wonder why anyone attempted to steal at all.

The success rate improved later in the decade, but Wills changed everything. With 104 steals in 117 attempts Wills success rate was 89%. Suddenly, stolen bases could be a big deal, and not just for runners, but for catchers. Weak armed catchers who could hit hadn't had any trouble finding a starting spot on a major league roster. Now they were seen as a liability. The next few years did not create a base stealing explosion as the myth goes, but that was partly due to the reaction of teams in response to Wills. There was a very large turnover in catchers in 1963, as catchers who could throw were now as valuable as catchers who could hit.

Another factor slowing down the increase in steals was the fact that baserunners still weren't very good at it.

It takes many qualities to be a good base-stealer. You must be fast, know how to get a good lead, have a good knowledge of pitchers and their idiosyncrasies, and have good judgment and confidence. Speed is inherent, but everything else must be learned.

So did Maury Wills usher in a new era of base stealing? Well, kinda, sorta. He certainly ushered in a new era of catchers, and as more and more fast black players entered the league, stolen bases were on everyone's mind more than they had been for many decades.

Still, the answer is not a simple one. Wills thought speed was a very important component of a successful team. It's no surprise that a base stealer would attribute greater importance to his skill, just as a homerun hitter might overemphasize the importance of power or a skilled shortstop the importance of defense. That's what we all do. Base stealers will argue that their mere presence on the base paths causes more stress on infielders and, especially, pitchers and while that cannot be measured, it is important. I think that theory is overrated.

For a somewhat different perspective, one National League umpire working in 1962 claimed that Wills had cost the Dodgers the pennant. How so, you ask? Junior Gilliam, batting after Wills, making an effort to give Wills every opportunity to steal, didn't swing at a lot of good pitches that he might otherwise have turned into hits and even more runs than Wills was generating.

One more comment. In 1965, in an attempt to break his own record, Wills was stealing bases at a faster rate than in 1962. That slowed significantly as the season wore on and he ended up with 94 steals. His body couldn't hold up to another assault on the record. Wills felt you should take the biggest lead possible. If you weren't diving back into the bag, your lead was too small. This led to a lot of pickoff throws and a lot of dives back into the base. Lou Brock eventually perfected the "rolling lead" creating more momentum to second base while not being far enough off the bag to entice many throws from the pitcher. There's a reason why great all-round ballplayers don't steal a lot of bases after the age of 25: the risk of injury is too great. Willie Mays, Hank Aaron, Barry Bonds and Ken Griffey Jr. could have easily stolen 50 bases a season up to age 30, but why would you risk it? My 40 homerun, 100 RBI guy is out of the lineup for a month because I asked him to steal a base? Managers may not have known advanced analytics, but they knew what would get them fired.

Jimmy Arias

Modern tennis is played with a speed and power and athleticism beyond the imagination of any player from the 1970s. Equipment has played a part, but it all started with Jimmy Arias and his father's vision of how the game could be played.

Tony Arias was a Cuban immigrant who settled in Grand Island, New York, just outside of Buffalo. He taught each of his three sons to play tennis, but his middle son Jimmy was by far the best.

Tony was an engineer without any formal tennis training. He taught Jimmy from an engineer's perspective. People entrenched in a sport are not usually the ones to bring a new perspective to it. Tony looked at the traditional forehand and envisioned hitting it in a new way. This is what he taught to Jimmy.

Jimmy's game was built around his forehand. His forehand was built around his father's idea of creating much more racquet head speed and much more topspin on the ball. This combination produced a faster shot that stayed inside the baseline and exploded off the ground up into the opponent, usually above his comfort zone.

What everyone else saw was a skinny kid whose body rotated wildly while his racquet whipped under and up through the ball far faster than they were used to.

With a weapon like this, you wanted to hit as many forehands as possible. Rather than hitting forehands on the right side of the court and backhands on the left side, Jimmy would attempt to hit as many forehands as he could. This often put him in the backhand corner hitting forehands. Conventional wisdom says you are compromising your court position too much by standing so far to one side to hit the ball. Tony Arias says "What does it matter where you're standing when you are crushing the ball?" Powerful offensive shots elicit weak returns, if the ball is returned at all. Giving up a little court position is a small price to pay.

Jimmy rolled through the junior tournaments wherever he played. Some Buffalo tennis players reached out to Buffalonian Murph Klauber, who was part owner of the "Colony Beach and Tennis Resort" in Sarasota, FL to give Jimmy a week of practice, and hopefully an opportunity to play year round against the best competition. They didn't think he could achieve his full potential staying in Buffalo.

While holding his own with bigger, stronger, top juniors he caught the attention of Nick Bolletieri, who was teaching at the Colony at the time.

Nick had the idea of taking a group of talented juniors and focusing on their tennis above all else. He needed someone like Jimmy Arias as a poster boy for his system.

Tony wanted Jimmy to train in Spain. Jimmy wanted to go with Nick in Florida. Jimmy eventually won and went to Florida and lived with Bolletieri. At 16, two years after he moved in with Bolletieri, Arias turned professional.

Jimmy's breakout year was 1983 at the age of 19. He stormed through the clay court season winning in Florence, Italy, the Italian Open in Rome and in Indianapolis, IN. In the 1983 U.S. Open in New York he lost in the semifinals to eventual champion Ivan Lendl after defeating French Open champion Yannick Noah in the quarterfinals.

He reached #5 in the world in 1984, his highest ranking. Four of his five career titles were in 1983. He retired in 1994 with a career record of 283-222. He is now a tennis commentator for several networks.

When Jimmy turned pro, there were almost no players, and certainly none of prominence, who hit the ball the way he did or positioned themselves on the court the way he did. Now, to some degree or other, they all do.

Nick Bolletieri, like Tony Arias, was not a tennis traditionalist, having come late to the game and not in the traditional way. He was smart enough not to try to change Jimmy's game. Others may not have been so open-minded.

Conversely, Jimmy arrived in Florida with a tremendous forehand, a winner's confidence, a mediocre backhand, weak serve and no volley. He emerged from Bolletieri Tennis Academy older, stronger, and still with a tremendous forehand, mediocre backhand, weak serve and no volley. Was he well served? I don't know.

Dick Fosbury

Eponymous:
"of, relating to, or being the person for which something is named."

Dick Fosbury, of Medford, OR, through a series of trial and error experiments became a high jumper when it was determined he wasn't very good at most other athletic endeavors. The problem was, he wasn't a very good high jumper either.

The prevailing high jump techniques of the day, the straddle and the less-popular scissors technique, did not allow him to jump very high. Slowly, he transformed the straddle technique, where he looked down at the bar, into one where he went over the bar backwards.

It was not a technique designed by physicists or exercise physiologists or track coaches for that matter. It just kinda evolved. An even quicker evolution was the naming of the jump. Whatever else it was called, the only name that mattered was the "Fosbury Flop."

He landed on his back, not his neck, but even that seemed dangerous. For those who study innovation and its origins, Fosbury was aided by what they call "the adjacent possible." The "adjacent possible" are concurrent events or inventions or discoveries which now allow your innovation to happen. In this case, it is a three foot thick square of foam rubber, covered in canvas that makes the Fosbury Flop survivable. Previously, high jumpers landed on a bed of sawdust or wood shavings. Landing on your back, or possibly your shoulders or neck, onto a pile of sawdust is no way to reach adulthood.

Winner of the NCAA high jump, he worked his way on to the 1968 U.S. Olympic Team. A novelty when the games began, Fosbury won the cheers of the crowd along with the Gold Medal in Mexico City with a jump of 7'4 ¼" and exposed "The Flop" to the world.

Despite his success, plenty of skeptics remained. Even his coach, Berny Wagner said "You can teach it to a 5' 6" jumper and in two weeks he will be jumping 5' 10". Of course, it may just be a shortcut to mediocrity!"??

The question mark is mine. He goes on to say "It's simpler in the air, more fluid in the pivot, allowing you to run harder, decelerating less and it may be more powerful from the ground."

In my limited understanding of the high jump, these all appear to be good things. The "unwillingness to accept the new" battles against reason until the battle is hopelessly lost.

In 1977, ten years later, a young high jumper, Volodya Yashchenko, reached prominence while jumping with the old straddle style. The consensus now was that the flop technique had gained acceptance not only because of Fosbury's success, but because it was easier to learn. There was an argument to be made for the straddle technique's ultimate superiority, but it was moot as almost all jumpers now were floppers, it being easier to learn.

Dick Fosbury, these days working as an engineer overseeing construction projects, didn't see himself as an innovator. "I just find different solutions to problems. I'm a problem solver. That's what engineers do."

Curiously, very few sports fans can identify Dick Fosbury, but most know the "Fosbury Flop!"

Football
Innovators

Football Innovators

"If you want something new,
you have to stop doing something old."

Peter Drucker

Unlike a lot of team sports, football is highly specialized. Long gone are the days when players played offense and defense. Paul Hornung in the 1960s was the last triple threat (run, pass and kick). Nowadays there are even specialties within specialties. "He's a pass defense linebacker" or a "3rd down" running back". The players that follow helped bring that about by being so good at one particular skill that they completely disrupted the other team. They said, "Forget about the past. This is how we play this position now."

John Mackey
TIGHT END

Before there was Gronk, before there was Antonio Gates, before there was Kellen Winslow there was John Mackey. Before John Mackey tight ends were almost offensive tackles. The game was more of a running game and tight ends were primarily blockers. Sure they could catch a ten yard pass over the middle for a first down but you had better be able to block.

John Mackey was from Roosevelt, NY and played football at Syracuse University. He was 6' 2" and 225 lbs and could run. He was the first tight end who was a true offensive weapon. If he couldn't outrun you, he could run over you. One year six of his nine touchdowns were for more than 50 yards. That was unheard of. Linebackers couldn't keep up with him and defensive backs couldn't bring him down.

As the game became more and more a passing game, tight ends were looked upon as receivers first, blockers second. Scouts were now looking for tight ends who could run and catch, like John Mackey. They were out there, but few were as good at it as Mackey.

John Mackey played nine seasons for the Baltimore Colts and one season for the San Diego Chargers, retiring after the 1972 season.

Unfortunately, Mr. Mackey was one of the first football players to develop severe cognitive difficulties in middle age, although no definitive causes were diagnosed in his lifetime.

He passed away in 2011 at the age of 70. The NFL Players Association created the "88" Plan to help ex-NFL players who required living assistance in their later years. Upon his death Mackey was found to have CTE, chronic traumatic encephalopathy, caused by too much trauma to the brain, probably as a result of too many hits to the head on the football field.

Pete Gogolak

PLACEKICKER

Pete Gogolak was signed by the Buffalo Bills in 1964, becoming the first soccer-style kicker in pro football. I realize there was not a lot of soccer being played in the U.S. in the 1950s and 60s but didn't anyone ever watch a soccer game? It would have been obvious that kicking with the side of the foot was superior to kicking with the toe, both for distance and for accuracy.

It's surprising that it took a kid who'd emigrated from Hungary and had not been exposed to American football to improve the kicking style, but that's what it took. I'm also sure that the first time he kicked that way, his coach tried to change him.

It wasn't long before everyone had a soccer style kicker with the exception of the New Orleans Saints who still relied on the deformed right foot of Tom Dempsey. League wide, accuracy increased, field goal distance increased and kickers became a much more valuable part of a football team's offensive repertoire. No longer were they position players who also kicked.

The Kansas City Chiefs won a Super Bowl in 1970 with an offense built around the idea that every time they crossed midfield their great kicker Jan Stenerud was in field goal range. 50-yard field goal attempts now made sense, especially when the dead ball was placed on the 20 yard line after a miss. They either got three points or the same result as a decent punt, a "can't lose" scenario.

Multiple rule changes have come in since to make the field goal attempt less desirable. First, they moved the goal posts to the back of the endzone. Then they took away the touchback on missed kicks and instead gave the other team the ball at the line of scrimmage of the kicking team and finally, returned the ball to the spot of the kick. Extra points became so automatic that they moved the ball back to the 20 yard line, which made for several misses per team on average, instead of maybe one a season. Of course they moved the kickoff line back based on the increased strength of the kickers, from the 40 yd line to the 35 and then the 30 until they decided that kickoffs were too dangerous and moved it back to the 35.

Unlike the quarterback position which always seems in short supply, it's been a long time since there has been a shortage of quality kickers. Thank you Mr. Gogolak.

While Pete Gogolak surely ushered in the flood of soccer style kickers, he wasn't particularly good at it himself. His field goal percentage from 40-49 yards away was only 36%. Compare that to contemporary straight on kicker Jim Bakken who had a 46% success rate at that distance. No wonder the Buffalo Bills owner Ralph Wilson thought that soccer style was the wrong way to kick a football and released him.

Things jumped quickly after that with Gary Anderson, a 20-year veteran from the 1980s until 2004 kicking at 71% and current longtime kicker Adam Vinatieri at 77% at that 40-49 yd distance.

The latest on the kicking scene now comes from Australia, where Australian Rules Football requires a variety of kicks and has produced some quality NFL punters.

The "drop" punt used by the Australians produces a kick with a much more controllable and predictable bounce and is especially effective at keeping kicks from bouncing into the endzone for a touchback.

This year's finalists for the top punter in college football were all Australians.

Even in football, a game played only by Americans, the world beyond our shores has something to teach us.

Deion Sanders
CORNERBACK

The 1972 Miami Dolphins averaged 18 passes with 10 completions on their way to an undefeated season. When the 2007 New England Patriots went undefeated, quarterback Tom Brady averaged 36 passes and 25 completions. Running the football became secondary to passing the football, and the trend had been growing for a long time.

At one time, cornerbacks had to be versatile enough to cover wide receivers and strong and skilled enough to shut down running plays to their side of the field. That versatility became less important as the balance between running and passing started to leave the offensive playbook.

What is now required is a cornerback who can cover the best receiver on the other team one-on-one. Deion, a two-time All-American at Florida State in 1987 and '88 was the first "shutdown" corner, a player you could put on the other team's top receiver and not have to worry about him. He was a truly gifted three sport All-State star in high school in Fort Myers, Florida and good enough to be drafted by major league baseball. With Deion guarding a receiver, there was no need to double team, no need to shade the safety to that side. The fact that he wasn't a great tackler barely rated a mention.

Deion was also a two sport player, playing baseball for the Atlanta Braves and then the Cincinnatti Reds while playing football for the Atlanta Falcons, San Francisco 49ers and Dallas Cowboys. The defenses these teams employed were not particularly complicated for someone whose only job was to cover the other team's best receiver. He could quickly go from baseball to football without the need for a full training camp. Like the other three gamechangers in this section, he increased the financial value of anyone who could do his job.

"Reivis Island" is the nickname for that part of the field where cornerback Darelle Reivis plays and that's a pretty good name as he is all alone, defending one on one. Reivis and cornerbacks like Josh Norman of Carolina now command big contracts for their ability to take away another team's best receiver, often their primary weapon.

Eventually, running the ball will come back in vogue and cornerbacks will have to tackle again, but that day now seems quite far away. Until it comes to pass, defending an elite wide receiver will remain a very valuable skill.

Lawrence Taylor
LINEBACKER

"My career didn't end when I broke my leg. My career ended when Lawrence Taylor broke my leg."
Joe Theismann

One of the more popular sports movies of recent times is "The Blind Side", which tells the story of Michael Ohr, a left tackle and eventual first-round pick of the Baltimore Ravens.

The opening shows the sacking, and the leg breaking of Joe Theisman, by Giants linebacker Lawrence Taylor. Never before had pro football seen such a devastatingly disruptive force as Lawrence Taylor and they really haven't seen one since.

What they have seen are linebackers who play almost like defensive ends, rushing the passer on almost every down. Dealing with them has not been easy and, as the movie suggests, left offensive tackles have become a whole lot more valuable because of it.

Until Taylor joined the New York Giants from the University of North Carolina in 1981, linebackers were linebackers and defensive ends were defensive ends. Linebackers occasionally rushed the passer but more often than not were part of the pass defense. Defensive ends, in the classic three point stance, defended against the run and always rushed the passer on pass plays. Nice and orderly. Everybody knows what everybody is supposed to be doing.

Lawrence Taylor put an end to all that. From his standup stance and linebacker position, he rushed the passer relentlessly. Even if he didn't rush on every pass play, he had to be accounted for as he was very gifted at finding the quarterback and very hard to elude.

Once again, like Deion Sanders, a player's ability to defend the passing game took priority over his ability to stop the run. Not that Taylor wasn't adept at going side to side to cover the run, but everyone was more concerned about his ability to run straight to the quarterback, the one man no pro football offense can afford to lose.

Players like Kevin Greene of the Pittsburgh Steelers, Clay Matthews of the Green Bay Packers, and DeMarcus Ware of Dallas and Denver commanded very large salaries based on their ability to rush the passer.

The video of Joe Theisman's leg breaking under the stress of being forced into a position it was never meant to be in is every coach's nightmare, not to be repeated under penalty of job loss, for as every coach knows "Lose your quarterback, lose your season!"

Trailblazers

Trailblazers

"The first one through the wall always gets bloodied."
John W. Henry, owner of the Boston Red Sox in the movie "Moneyball"

Part I. The Foreigners

Someone has to be first, just to prove it can be done. It may take others to prove that it can be done well, but someone has to do it first. This group of athletes is among the first to break through in their sport and also the first to show that they belong at the elite levels of their sport.

European hockey players had played in the NHL at various times, but most American hockey fans only remembered the famous game between the mighty Soviet Red Army team and the Philadelphia Flyers.

The Red Army team walked off the ice in protest after a body check to Valeri Kharmalov was not called a penalty. Kharmalov lay on the ice for more than a minute and when he got up the Soviet team left the ice.

When they finally returned, under the threat of not getting paid, the Flyers continued their assault and outscored the Red Army 4-1 and outshot them 49-13.

This confirmed what every red-blooded American and Canadian hockey fan knew, that European hockey players were too soft to play in the NHL.

European basketball players did not play defense and were not skilled enough to compete in the NBA. Didn't college players beat up on them in the Olympics every four years? How could they compete with the pros?

The Ladies Professional Golf Association (LPGA) was a tour for Americans only for most of its existence. Always struggling for the success the men's tour had achieved, they got a publicity bump when Annika Sorenstam arrived from Sweden and quickly became recognized as the best female golfer in the world. Annika was super talented, but no threat to the existing order. Would the next invader be different?

Sports in the United States in the 1950s and 60s was strictly played, watched and cared about only in the U.S. With the exception of the Olympics every four years, nothing that occurred anywhere else in the world was of the least concern.

The only film ever available from European sporting events arrived by plane and was at least 12 hours old. Europeans didn't play baseball and football and weren't very good at basketball. The British Open in golf wasn't a very big deal since most American golfers didn't make the trip because expenses ate up any prize earnings. In those days, winning a major wasn't automatically worth millions.

With the exception of the occasional European golfer, Latin American baseball player or Australian tennis player, American sports were for Americans. We didn't care about the rest of world and the rest of the world didn't care about us. Why should they? We didn't play soccer. If it weren't for boxing and track and field our athletes would have been completely unknown to them.

Still, the lure of more money and a chance to compete against the best kept the foreigners knocking on the door. These are the ones who knocked it down.

Borje Salming

In 1972 the World Hockey Association was formed to challenge the NHL and a search for talent was on. Until that time, the league was almost entirely Canadian. After 1972, Americans and Europeans, particularly Swedes, starting pouring into the league. The best of these was Borje Salming, a big defenseman who played 16 seasons in the NHL, almost all of them with the Toronto Maple Leafs. He also starred in international events for Sweden. He remains the Maple Leafs career leader in assists and was the first European NHL All-Star.

Not a fighter like most North American defensemen, he could still check and take a check with the very best of them, eventually earning the respect of players and fans alike.

He was so loved in Toronto that while playing for the Swedish National Team against Team USA in the 1976 Canada Cup in Toronto, he received a standing ovation in the introductions, as if he were a beloved native Canadian.

Upon his retirement from the NHL he continued to play in his native Sweden.

Inducted into the Hockey Hall of Fame in 1997, he was the first great European star in the NHL. Many others would follow. Eventually the Czechs and Russians would leave their Communist countries behind and come to North America to make their fortune.

Meanwhile, on the other side of the continent....

The Russians are coming! The Russians are coming! Actually, it's the Lithuanians.

Arvydas Sabonis and Sarunas Marciulonis

The 1988 Seoul Olympics would be yet another chance to show U.S. dominance in basketball. Other teams could play their so-called "amateurs" but NBA players were barred. No matter, with future NBA greats David Robinson, Mitch Richmond and Danny Manning on the team, the U.S. would have no trouble again beating the world. With the exception of the extremely controversial game against the Soviet Union in 1972, the U.S. had never been beaten.

Soviet Union 76 – United States 68.

What the hell just happened?

A trio of Lithuanians, Sarunas Marciulonis, Arvydas Sabonis and Rimas Kurtinaitis led the Soviet Union to one of the greatest basketball upsets in history. From 1992 on, the U.S. was able to use NBA players, and while the rest of the world has begun to catch up, no one nation can field a team as good and as deep as the USA.

With the breakup of the Soviet Union, Marciulonis and Sabonis were able to leave Europe to come play in the NBA. Marciulonis joined the Golden State Warriors in 1989 and played in the NBA until 1997, twice winning Sixth Man of the Year Awards. He has been a mainstay of the Lithuanian and European basketball establishment ever since.

Arvydas Sabonis did not come to the Portland Trailblazers until 1995 and played until 2003. Sabonis did not reach the NBA until he was 31, slowed by many knee and leg injuries. He still managed to average 16.0 points and 10.0 rebounds in 97-98. It is generally agreed that had he reached Portland in his prime, they would have won many NBA titles. A hypothetical title is easy to achieve and very hard to take away.

These guys began the march of German, Dutch, Serbian and Croatian players who have steadily crossed the ocean to play against America's best. he French jumped in with Tony Parker, Boris Diaw and Rudy Gobert along with the Turks, Hedo Turkoglu and Omer Asik. Even the Turks, Hedo Turkoglu and Omer Asik, got into the act.

The latest invasion is now from South America with stars like Nene' and Manu Ginobli and a trickle of Australians like Andrew Bogut and Paddy Mills. The Chinese even tipped a toe into the ocean and sent Yao Ming over.

Though no Japanese players have made it to the NBA, Japan still got into the act.

Hideo Nomo

In 1995 Japan's Hideo Nomo made his debut as a Los Angeles Dodger, becoming the first player from Japan since Masanori Murakami pitched for the San Francisco Giants 30 years earlier. Murakami pitched less than 100 innings in two seasons and was forced to return to Japan after the 1965 season.

Nomo, using a loophole in his contract, signed with the Los Angeles Dodgers as a free agent and pitched in the U.S. from 1995-2008.

He was an immediate success with the Dodgers on and off the field, leading the league in strikeouts, pitching a no-hitter and winning the National League Rookie of the Year. Off the field he created the same furor with the Amer-asian population that Fernando Valenzuela had done with the Hispanic population in 1981.

In an up and down career he won 123 games and paved the way for other Japanese stars to come to America. Ichiro Suzuki, Hidecki Matsui and Daisuke Matsuzaka all followed Nomo.

While this was undoubtedly good for Major League Baseball it wasn't nearly as good for Japanese baseball, as its most important stars were coming to the U.S.

Sadahara Oh, the Babe Ruth of Japan, would not have been as revered as he is to this day in Japan had he decided to play in the U.S.A. in his prime.

Still, Nomo proved that Japanese ballplayers could be very successful in the U.S. and the lure of larger contracts and the chance to play against the very best has sent a steady stream of them across the Pacific to this day. Currently there are eight on major league rosters and a total of 52 have played since Hideo Nomo first pitched in 1995.

Chan Ho Park

Chan Ho Park was the first South Korean to play in the majors. Making his debut for the L.A. Dodgers at the age of 20 in 1994, Chan pitched seven seasons for the Dodgers and 17 overall, amassing 124 wins against 98 losses. 19 South Koreans have followed Chan to the majors, but so far he has been the best.

The ladies were also not immune from this invasion.

Se Ri Pak

South Korea seems like an unlikely place to produce large quantities of professional female golfers. There are not a lot of golf courses in South Korea, approximately 200, compared to over 15,000 in the U.S. However, there are a lot of driving ranges. And there is Se Ri Pak.

Born in 1977 she joined the U.S. LPGA Tour in 1998 as a 20-year old and proceeded to win two majors, the U.S. Open, and the McDonald's LPGA Championship before her 21st birthday. Three more majors and a total of 39 tournament wins got her into the World Golf Hall of Fame at the tender age of 29, youngest living entrant ever.

With the quick success came great fame and great pressure from sponsors and an adoring Korean public. The stress was at times overwhelming and it showed in her golf.

From 1998 to 2004 she was in the top three in earnings 5 out of 6 years. She made the cut in majors 28 consecutive times before failing in the 2005 U.S. Open. In 2005 her best finish was a tie for 27th. Unhappy with her golf and her life, she needed to find some balance, which she subsequently did, returning to take the 2006 LPGA Championship for the third time.

Pak continued on tour for another 10 years, successful if not spectacular.

Meanwhile, back in South Korea, young girls began hitting golf balls in record numbers and following Se ri onto the U.S. LPGA Tour. A recent count found 45 South Korean female golfers on the LPGA Tour, nearly 40% of the top 100, surpassed only by the U.S.

This has caused a few problems for the tour as the press guide is now filled with Parks, Paks, Kims and Jins. Many of the girls speak very little English, making TV interviews less than ideal. The Pro-Am events designed to give local club officials and tournament sponsors more contact with the players loses some of its appeal when all conversation happens through an interpreter. The tour even briefly considered an English language requirement but thought better of it. To put the Korean phenomenon in perspective, Sweden's Annika Sorenstam won 72 tour events and 10 majors and was undoubtedly the best of her generation, but only three Swedish golfers are now ranked in the top 100.

It's not hard to imagine a country like South Korea, small and prosperous, coming out every four years and dominating some obscure Olympic sport like archery or air rifle, particularly among the women. But golf? Golf, which requires acres and acres to even play a game? Golf, which really has no Asian tradition? Golf?

And yet, there it is. 45 of the top 100 in the world hail from South Korea, and we owe it all to Se ri Pak.

Part II: The Americans

From the late 1960s all the way back to the beginning, college basketball didn't let freshmen compete with the varsity. Apparently, besides letting them adjust to college life, freshmen weren't physically ready to compete at the varsity level. Besides, the pros wouldn't draft you until your class graduated so there was plenty of time to show off your skills.

Sooner or later that notion was going to be tested. In 1968 for most sports, and for football and basketball in 1972, freshmen could now play on the varsity.

The original reasoning was that it was a cost-cutting move, eliminating the need for a freshman or Junior varsity team. Others claimed it was to exploit these young athletes for a full four years.

But there was a war on between the NBA and the ABA. While truth may be the first casualty of war, youth isn't very far behind.

When a slight 6'10" 18 year old from Petersburg, Virginia agreed to go to the Maryland Terrapins basketball team, coach Lefty Driesell cleared a place on his mantle for the NCAA Championship Trophy.

Unbeknownst to poor old Lefty, the Utah Stars of the ABA had just offered that young man $1,000,000 to play professional basketball right out of high school. And that's how

Moses Malone

became one of the richest eighteen year olds in the country.

The NFL and NBA had forced kids into college because they wouldn't draft them until their college class had graduated. The NCAA loved this as they kept their stars for four years and the pros got mature young men who they thought they knew something about. Soon they were getting very talented but immature juveniles who they didn't know a thing about.

In 1971, Spencer Haywood, Olympic star and standout player at the University of Detroit sued for the right to work in the NBA just like any other job. The league and the courts agreed to let any player who could prove a financial hardship by being kept out of the league apply for the draft. This is the door Moses Malone walked through.

Picked in the third round by the Utah Stars, Moses signed a five-year $1,000,000 contract. He was an ABA All-Star in his first season. He went on to a Hall of Fame ABA-NBA career, winning three MVP Awards, one NBA Championship, and nine rebounding titles. A thirteen time All-Star, he was inducted into the Hall of Fame in 2001.

Shortly after Moses signed a contract with the pros, Daryll Dawkins, aka "Chocolate Thunder", signed with the Philadelphia 76ers. In the second round of the same draft, Bill Willoughby signed with the Atlanta Hawks. Neither Dawkins nor Willoughby lived up to their perceived potential and that's why it took 20 years for Kevin Garnett to be drafted out of a Chicago high school.

Of course, the success of Garnett started a whole slew of high school draftees. Many teams, desperately in need of better players, were forced to draft a talented but unknown 18 year old. Many did not fulfill expectations, leaving many a struggling NBA franchise to struggle some more. Finally, the NBA and the Players Association agreed to not draft anyone before the age of 19 and one year out of high school. This began with the 2006 draft.

Now young hoop stars go to college or the University of Kentucky (famous for freshmen who turn pro after one year) to wait a year for the NBA draft. This so called "one and done" isn't particularly liked by the NCAA or the NBA but it serves as a compromise everyone can live with.

Not only are young people trying to crack into pro sports, but, can you believe it, women are trying to compete with men!

Women couldn't compete with men in "ANY" sport. Hell, they couldn't compete with them at anything else, either, or so the men would have you believe.

Women do not compete with men in very many sports. With the exception of some highly skilled sports like trap shooting, archery and billiards, women aren't strong enough, fast enough or big enough to compete with men. Some thought they could compete with men as jockeys, but no one would give them a chance, until someone did.

Diane Crump

"Live your dream. Don't let anyone tell you that you can't or that you're not good enough. You are. I'm a little nobody, yet I'm in a history book. I didn't plan on that. All I did was follow my passion, the gift that God gave me, and I never let it die."

Diane Crump

Women had been prevented from becoming jockeys since forever. In the 1960s a few had been issued licenses but no one actually rode in a sanctioned pari-mutuel race until Diane Crump on February 7th 1969 at Hialeah Race Track in Florida. She again made news in 1970 when she became the first female jockey to ride in the Kentucky Derby on a horse named "Phantom," finishing 15th of 17.

Despite suffering all the indignities of any pioneer, she persevered and rode 236 winners until she retired in 1985. Never receiving the best mounts, she had little opportunity to reach the pinnacle of her sport. The knock on women was that they weren't strong enough to compete at the highest levels and weren't good finishers.

Diane's response to this criticism was to point out that no 110 lb human has the strength to control a 1200-lb horse, if strength is all you have. It takes so much more.

Male jockeys were indifferent to her at best, cruel at worst.

As Bobby Cox, Brooklyn teammate of Jackie Robinson put it when he discovered that Negro Junior Gilliam would be replacing him at third base "How would you like to lose your job to a N-----r?"

For "N-----r" just substitute any pejorative for female you choose and that's what Diane Crump heard all the time. One Hall of Fame jockey claimed he would give up riding if he lost to her.

Now a grandmother of two and 63 years old, she still receives hundreds of letters a year from young girls asking what it was like to be the first? "When I got my exercise license at 16, there were no girls working either as grooms or exercise riders. Now about 50% of backstretch help is female.

Many followed Diane into the jockey ranks with varying degrees of success. Patty Barton and Mary Bacon quickly followed and rode with success, but at minor tracks. Donna Barton Brothers, Patty's daughter, won 1,130 races while riding for trainers like D. Wayne Lukas, winner of four Kentucky Derbys. She even finished 2nd in a Breeder's Cup race, but none were at the top level of the sport, until

Julie Krone

"There is a presence, a conscious unconsciousness that an athlete can produce something without explanation."
Julie Krone

Julie Krone, standing 5' nuthin' and just over a hundred pounds, rode her first winner at Tampa Bay Downs in February 1981 and went on to become leading rider at major tracks like the Meadowlands, Monmouth Park, Gulfstream Park and Belmont Park.

She became the first female winner of a Triple Crown race winning the Belmont Stakes aboard Colonial Affair in 2000, and the first winner of a Breeder's Cup race in 2003 aboard Halfbridled.

Riding with the best of the best in New York and California, she was a winner of numerous Grade I stakes races, and consistently in the top 10 in earnings for more than a decade. In 1993 she received an ESPY as Female Athlete of the Year. In 2000 she was inducted into the Racing Hall of Fame, the first female jockey to be so honored. Injuries forced her into retirement in 2004. While women had now been jockeys for 40 years, only Julie Krone had been elite. Was she a fluke? The answer seemed to be "yes" until the arrival of

Rosie Napravnik

"We are beyond the days of being boycotted. We are beyond the days before Civil Rights. So it has to do with the woman. It has to do with the individual and being able to compete as smart, as sharp as any man.
Rosie Napravnik 2014

Rosie Napravnik began her riding career in 2005 at the age of 17 under the name "A. R. Napravnik" so as not to give away her gender. Eventually she became just "Rosie" as she led racing meets at Laurel Racecourse and Pimlico in Maryland, the Fairgrounds in New Orleans and the prestigious Keeneland Race Course in Kentucky. Along the way she broke the record for earnings by a female jockey and won a couple of Breeder's Cup Races.

Finishing in the top ten in earnings from 2012-2014, Rosie retired from racing after the 2014 Breeder's Cup to begin a family. She won 1,877 races from 9,715 mounts or nearly 20%. Her mounts earned over $71,000,000 in a very short career.

While she is unquestionably one of the top riders of her generation, she also proved that Julie Krone was no fluke and that women could compete at the top levels of the sport. Women make up only 10% of jockeys and continue to face prejudice from male trainers and male jockeys.

In all walks of life, discrimination can be expensive, as many an owner and trainer have discovered as the Julie Krones and Rosie Napravniks of the racing world dismounted in the Winner's Circle, unaware that they "weren't good enough!"

Science and Technology

Science and Technology

We live in an age of incredibly rapid technological change. Data that took years to accumulate at the beginning of the century is now gathered in a day. From the beginning of the 1950s until now is like night and day.

Very little film exists from the '50s, let alone video. Common computer usage was still 30 years away. Computers from 20 years ago are laughably obsolete. So it is with sports science. Those who were quick to recognize the advantages offered by technological change were rewarded with success. Those who denied it faced an uphill battle at best

This next group represents the leaders in this remarkable age.

Howard Head

*"Improvements can only be made by those
who feel something is not good."*
Friedrich Nietzsche

Howard Head was not a very good skier. Like many frustrated amateur sportsmen, he was more than willing to blame his equipment for his poor performance. Unlike the others, he set out to do something about it.

As an aerospace engineer he knew something about modern materials and design. He first set out to make a lighter, more maneuverable ski. His initial prototypes proved too fragile, but after a long period of trial and error, Head produced a somewhat lighter, far more maneuverable aluminum, plywood, plastic composite ski.

To reach the mass market, Head knew he had to get it to be used by ski instructors and professionals. By 1959, his skis were dominating the professional ranks. In 1969 he sold Head Ski to AMF for $16,000,000.

With his newfound windfall, Head bought a large house outside Baltimore and had a tennis court built so that he could get some exercise.

New sport, same result. Howard Head was not a very good tennis player. His instructor convinced him to get a ball machine so that he could get more practice.

Head was convinced his erratic hitting was the result of a poor racquet. Every hit that was slightly off-center (and there were many) caused the racquet to torque in his hand. This is why he sprayed so many shots. He knew he could increase his successful shots if he could increase the size of the racquet's sweet spot.

Up until this time, there had been very little innovation in tennis racquet design. Tennis, from the 1890s to the 1960s had been mostly a country club sport steeped in tradition and with a limited market for equipment. The major tournaments were limited to amateurs. Unlike golf, tennis professionals were shut out of the major events and forced to barnstorm around the country playing exhibitions in armories and high school gymnasiums. The "tour" was usually limited to the reigning professional and the winner of one of the previous year's big amateur events. There wasn't a lot of interest in changing the tennis racquet.

1968 and the first U.S. Open brought on the modern era of professional tennis and a soon to be explosion in interest in the sport. Many of the new enthusiasts quickly found out what Howard Head already knew; tennis was not as easy as it looked and the equipment didn't help much.

Head began his quest for a new racquet design with the idea that he had to increase the sweet spot. To do that, he would have to make the racquet wider. If it was wider, it would have to be taller and soon Howard had designed what looked like a snowshoe more than a tennis racquet.

One of the reasons the traditional racquet had not changed was that wood was not the strongest or lightest of materials and bigger racquets were either way too heavy or way too breakable to be viable. Head used an extruded aluminum tube for the frame which was light and durable and had a much larger sweet spot.

Many of the early adopters of the new racquet found significant improvement in their game including defeating opponents they had never beaten before. They also found scorn and ridicule for playing with such a big racquet.

The professionals who adopted the new equipment often saw a meteoric rise up the rankings and the floodgates were opened for new racquet designs with all kinds of new materials.

It took a while for wooden racquets to be completely replaced by the new frames, but the results were undeniable. Larger, lighter racquets were superior.

Nowadays, a conventional wooden racquet feels like a wooden club with a hitting surface barely larger than your palm. We wonder how we could ever have played with such things.

Howard Head was stubborn enough to believe that he was not the problem, it was his equipment, and stubborn enough to persevere through the trial and error process to produce a revolution in sports equipment. He was at the forefront of the tech revolution that was not just limited to equipment. Exercise physiology, computer analysis, and high-speed video were all just around the corner from Howard Head's workshop.

Other sports were also getting a technological bump, as it were. Golf clubs went from wooden shafts to steel to lighter metals to sophisticated composites and graphite. New head shapes like the "Big Bertha" driver or the extra long shaft of the "belly putter" were also experimented with.

Improved safety equipment for other sports was evolving. Goalie masks were creeping into the NHL with Jacques Plante being the first goalie to wear a mask full time in 1959. Helmets for the other players began to be worn throughout the league. Eventually they became mandatory but many of the older players insisted that they couldn't play in a helmet. I guess putting your brain at risk for a little comfort made a lot more sense. These players forced through a "grandfather" clause which allowed those already in the league to play without one for as long as they were in the league. Fortunately I could not find any record of one of these old-timers hitting their head and going into a coma.

Craig MacTavish, retiring after the 1996-97 season was the last to play without a helmet.

Football helmets were also improving, becoming stronger, lighter and more durable. Unfortuantely, with such protection, too many players began to use their head as a battering ram, causing immediate effects like concussions and long term effects like Traumatic Brain Injuries (TBI), to be discussed later. Top of the line football helmets now cost $400, and I'm not talking about the NFL.

Dr. Frank Jobe and Tommy John

"The best players in any high-stakes field – business, entertainment, law, surgery, as well as sport – recognize that pressure occurs at the moments when meaningful accomplishment is possible. In fact, that is the reason why performers perform: for the opportunity to tackle challenges head on, to do something significant, to demonstrate what their hard work and talent can produce."

John Eliot

Sports are not immune from the outside world and one of the areas that has exploded in our lifetimes is modern medicine. One of the reasons that the expense of healthcare is such a recent, but pressing, problem is that medicine can do lots and lots of things to help you live a longer, better life.

When my grandfather had a heart attack, he was rushed to the hospital where the doctor told him "You've had a heart attack." He stayed in the hospital a few days and was told that the next heart attack would probably kill him, which it did. Not very helpful, but not very expensive either.

Nowadays, a stress test would have revealed his problem and he either would have been treated with drugs, had a stent implanted, had bypass surgery or been put on the list for a heart transplant. See how much more we can do, and how much more expensive that all must be.

Athletes have been a big beneficiary of all the new diagnostic techniques, drug therapies, and surgical breakthroughs. Athletes can recover from previously career-ending injuries and modern training techniques can make the body much more durable.

In September of 1974 Dr. Frank Jobe suggested a surgery to a major league pitcher which he thought had a less than 2% chance of repairing what would have been a career-ending injury. The surgery was an Ulnar Collateral Ligament (UCL) reconstruction. The damaged ligament in the affected arm is replaced with a tendon from the other arm.

Despite less than rosy predictions, the procedure was a success and the pitcher pitched successfully for many more seasons. His name was Tommy John and everyone other than Dr. Jobe began calling the procedure "Tommy John" surgery. We are all fortunate that the first patient was someone with a melodic name like Tommy John rather than, for example, Duke's Mike Krzyzewski.

Dr. Jobe also performed the first successful shoulder reconstruction surgery on Hall of Fame pitcher Orel Hershiser.

It is estimated that in 2015, 128 ULC reconstruction surgeries will be performed on major and minor league ballplayers, the vast majority of them pitchers. Approximately two-thirds of those who have the surgery have full recoveries and can return to baseball.

At the time of Dr. Jobe's death in 2014, 124 active pitchers had had Tommy John surgery or one-third of all those pitching in the majors. That's an amazing number.

Knee injuries such as tears to the anterior cruciate ligament (ACL) and medial collateral ligament (MCL), common football injuries, used to be fatal to an athlete's career. Now players often recover and perform as well, or almost as well as prior to the injury. In fact, in the past, most surgery was career ending. Far less invasive surgery techniques also make recovery much easier. Many athletes now return from surgery in the same season. These and similar surgeries help athletes after their playing careers are over and the ravages of age begin to take their toll on bodies pushed to the max. We live in an age of medical marvels.

Victor Conte

Advancements have not just come on the surgical side of medicine. World-class performance can be enhanced even further by other means. As early as the 1960s anabolic steroids were starting to come into use for sports such as bodybuilding. A 6' 6" former high school basketball and football opponent of mine told me his college track coach, who had great success with his teams in the strength field events (discus, shot put, etc.), could make him the first 300 lb lineman in the NFL. He had the frame for it, he just didn't have the muscle. Apparently, that could be manufactured. (He declined the invitation.) Ben Johnson, as perfectly chiseled an athlete as you will ever meet, was disqualified from his world record setting performance in the 100m sprint at the Seoul Olympics in 1988 for steroid use. Scandalous at the time, but repeated many times since.

Welcome to Major League Baseball in the 1990s. In August of 1994 MLB began its longest work stoppage. The strike began on August 12, 1994 and lasted through the rest of the season, cancelling the playoffs and, for the first time since 1904, the World Series. 1995 started off no better, with the owners talking about using replacement players. On March 28th, 1995 the strike officially ended and a 144-game season was agreed upon.

Fans reacted to the strike and subsequent resumption of baseball with indifference. Attendance was way down as were television ratings. The one bright spot was Cal Ripken's assault on the legendary Lou Gehrig's ironman streak of playing in 2,130 consecutive games. Ripken's streak was the highlight of the 1995 season and on September 6th Ripken played in his 2,131st consecutive game, on his way to the new record of 2,630 games in a row.

1996, the first full season in three years, saw Mark McGuire lead the majors in homeruns with 52. The American League also hit 1.21 homers per game, the most in history. McGuire's next three seasons saw him hit 58 in 1997 (split between the Oakland A's and St. Louis Cardinals), 70 in 1998-shattering Roger Maris' 37-year-old record of 61, and 65 in 1999. Chasing McGuire was Sammy Sosa, who from 1998 to 2001, hit, 66, 63, 50, and 64 homeruns. Barry Bonds hit 73 homeruns in 2001 while appearing in only 153 games, a homer in every 2.1 games and a homerun in every 6.5 at-bats. In the previous 100 year history of the game only two men, Babe Ruth and Roger Maris, had hit 60 homeruns and now it had been done six times in four years. Baseball regained its popularity in an explosion of power.

Lurking in the shadows were rumors that, while the baseballs weren't juiced, the players might be. Sportswriters were noticing players returning to spring training with 15-20 lbs more muscle than they had left with at the end of the previous season. Some of them were even starting to write about it.

In March 2006 Baseball Commissioner Bud Selig commissioned former U.S. Senator George Mitchell to investigate illegal performance enhancing substances in baseball. In 2007 the Mitchell Report named some high profile players including Roger Clemens and Jason Giambi. It suggested that players on every major league roster were involved. Since testing had been very limited, steroid abuse was rampant. When Mark McGuire was mentioned as using androsteniodone (I can't pronounce it either), sales of this particular drug shot through the roof, used by athletes all the way down to the high school level.

The federal government focused its investigation into BALCO (Bay Area Laboratory Co-operative), a sports nutrition center run by Victor Conte. Conte is responsible for developing the steroid THG, administered as a "clear" cream. Through BALCO, sprinter Marion Jones, football player Bill Romanowski and Barry Bonds were implicated in steroid use. Romanowski had appeared on the news magazine "Sixty Minutes" touting his sports longevity and revitalization as a product of the nearly 200 vitamins he took daily. It wasn't the steroids?

....

"It's not cheating if everybody is doing it. And if you've got the knowledge that that's what everyone is doing, and those are the real rules of the game, then you're not cheating."

Victor Conte

....

Marion Jones won three gold medals and two bronze in track and field at the 2000 Summer Olympics in Sydney, Australia. Caught up in the Victor Conte, BALCO, scandal, she eventually admitted to steroid use. Stripped of her Olympic medals, she also served prison time for lying to federal agents.

Barry Bonds' career after the age of 34 was nothing less than fantastic. When most players begin or continue to decline, Bonds was hitting homeruns at an historic rate, culminating with 73 in 2001. It was also apparent that Bonds had gotten bigger, including his head, an indication that he may have been taking Human Growth Hormone (HGH). Eventually, in leaked Grand Jury testimony, Bonds admitted to using "the cream" and "the clear," two of Conte's creations, but not knowing they were steroids. As others have before him, he attributed his success to changes in diet, bodybuilding and vitamins.

As the architect of all this, Victor Conte eventually served four months in prison in return for full disclosure of his activities. Conte claims that passing drug tests is "like taking candy from a baby" and that the Olympics are as corrupt as anyone can imagine.

It is obvious that steroids help athletes. The argument in baseball had been that drugs and muscle can't help you hit a 98 mph fastball or a nasty curveball-and that may be true-, but they can help you hit it a lot farther.

The tennis argument had been that steroids wouldn't help you hit a better backhand, but in 2005 Mariano Puerta made the French Open Finals before losing to Rafael Nadal. Puerta, up to that time, had never made it to the third round of any Grand Slam event. Testing positive for the second time, Puerta received an eight year ban, effectively ending his pro tennis career.

Athletes know how helpful these drugs can be. Whether it is performance enhancing, recovery, or healing an injury, the effects are well known.

We also know that athletes will cheat, no matter what the supposed negative consequences down the road, and people like Victor Conte will be around to provide the latest and greatest iteration of these drugs.

If athletes will take health-threatening drugs to improve performance, can vague warnings of other possible damage deter them from pursuing their dreams?

In 2005 center Eddy Curry was leading the Chicago Bulls in scoring when he was sidelined with an irregular heartbeat. The Bulls wanted to give him a test for Hypertrophic Cardiomyopathy (HCM), a thickening of the left ventricle and the #1 cause of sudden death among young people and athletes.

Fearing that he might drop dead on the court, the Bulls offered to pay Curry $400,000 a year for 50 years if he took the test for (HCM) and was found with the identifying gene. Rather than give up his current $3,800,000 salary and a potential to double that, he refused the test. The Bulls traded him to the Knicks. Eddy Curry did not drop dead, but he did turn down $400,000 a year for fifty years and a ticket to a longer life just so he could play a little more ball. Authorized to play by other experts, Curry retired in 2013 and is alive and well.

This leads us to:

Dr. Bennett Omalu

*"We old athletes carry the disfigurements and markings of
contests remembered only by us and no one else. Nothing is more
lost than a forgotten game."*
Pat Conroy

Modern medicine can fix you if you are broken. Modern drugs can make you perform even better. But what if you are broken but don't know how or why?

Mike Webster was an NFL Hall of Fame Center for the Super Bowl-winning Pittsburgh Steelers of the 1970s. After a 17-year career, Webster's life post-football quickly devolved into a life of anger, depression, alcoholism, and homelessness. He died in 2002 at the age of 50.

An autopsy, performed on Webster by Dr. Bennett Omalu, a Nigerian pathologist with eight advanced degrees and a relatively recent arrival to this country, revealed a brain of someone much older, with indications of Alzheimer's or a severe brain injury. Research on other deceased former players with similar conditions revealed similar brains. Dr. Omalu named it Chronic Traumatic Encephalopathy, or CTE. It describes a brain that has been shaken inside the skull many, many times, often producing concussions, but not always.

It should be noted that the NFL often categorized these depressed, angry and suicidal ex-players as people who were not able to adjust to a post-pro football life. They had not adjusted to the loss of the adulation of 50,000 screaming fans, the celebrity, and the camaraderie of teammates. It was never suggested that perhaps the repeated head collisions of football could be at fault.

Dr. Omalu reached out to the NFL to do a much larger and more thorough study of players' brains but the NFL never responded.

The NFL, through its Mild Traumatic Brain Injury (MTBI) committee, headed by a rheumatologist (I can't make this stuff up!) produced several reports stating no long term injuries related to concussions.

"Players who are concussed and return to the same game have fewer initial signs and symptoms than those removed from play. Return to play does not involve a significant risk of a second injury either in the same game or during the season." (!!!!)

Neurologists, players, and continuing studies on head trauma, clearly contradicted the findings of the MTBI committee.

Dr. Omalu was threatened personally and professionally by those who thought he wanted to take football away. The NFL attempted to discredit him and his findings.

As more and more studies confirm the increased depression and neurological problems of retired players, more attention is being given to the way football is played and the proper treatment for those who suffer head trauma.

The suicide of former Chicago Bears safety Dave Duerson, the murder-suicide involving Kansas City Chief linebacker Jovan Belcher, and the suicide of San Diego Chargers linebacker Junior Seau brought a more intense scrutiny to the NFL and it's players.

The NFL now has a concussion protocol preventing players from returning to games in which they have suffered a concussion, and additional protocols before they can return to practice.

After stonewalling for years-using many of the same tactics and consultants as the tobacco industry, the NFL recently settled a lawsuit with 3,000 retired players for $765,000,000, a number which almost everyone but the NFL agrees is way too small to cover necessary treatment, but gives money to the ex-players now, rather than waiting far into the future.

Dr. Omalu is adamant that he wishes he had never met Mike Webster and that he has nothing against football, but thought that people should know the potential consequences of football collisions. Others realize the game changer this may be for the NFL. If kids stop playing football, youth participation is already down 10%, professional football may go the way of boxing. It might even take college and high school football with it.

The NFL has incorporated many rule changes in an attempt to make the game safer. Concussions still occur in abundance. Players are starting to take notice; many are retiring earlier than in the past, and some may follow the path of San Francisco Defensive Rookie of the year Chris Borland, who retired after one year in the league, concerned about the consequences of possible head trauma. Unfortunately, football is an inherently violent sport and that is much of what people like about it. We haven't come that far from ancient Rome and the gladiators. The modern gladiators just have better helmets with jazzier logos.

The gene ApoE 4 makes recovery from head trauma more difficult. If from one parent, three times more difficult, if from two parents 8 times more difficult. 2% of people have two copies of the gene. Currently, neither the NCAA nor the NFL test for this gene.

Bill James and the Analytics Revolution

"What gets measured, gets managed."
Peter Drucker, management guru

"Analytics is something invented by guys who couldn't play sports but wanted to be involved in sports so they could still get the girls."
Charles Barkley and Shaquille O'Neal on their
Emmy winning TNT show "At the Half" about NBA basketball

Just as the legends of so many inventors begin with one man in his garage, the legend of Bill James begins on the night shift at the Stokely – Van Camp's pork and beans factory where James' early writings on baseball began. James challenged baseball orthodoxy with questions like "Are batting average, RBIs and Won-Lost record the best way to evaluate players? Do pitchers who strike out fewer batters than average have as long a career as those who strike out an above average number of hitters? Do white ballplayers lose their speed earlier than black ballplayers?" Armed with only box scores from the newspaper and whatever published statistics were available, James set out to answer these and many other questions.

In an 80 page report sold through *The Sporting News* in 1977, James found a few other like-minded baseball statistic aficionados and Sabermetrics (Society for American Baseball Research (SABR)), an umbrella term for advanced baseball statistics, was born.

Through the years James and his peers created a whole group of new statistics in an attempt to better explain the game. Baseball chose to ignore these analytics - and James. Like Barkley and O'Neal quoted above, they couldn't believe that these outsiders could possibly understand the game as well as those who had played it at the highest levels.

They included everyone except Billy Beane, General Manager of the Oakland Athletics who, in 1998, had to compete with the Boston Red

Sox and New York Yankees with a payroll only a third of those teams. When that's the situation, you should be willing to look at the game in a different way from the rich teams, because you can't compete if you attempt to do what they do.

Beane's success, chronicled in Michael Lewis's excellent book "Moneyball" and the movie by the same name, started to turn the heads of those in positions of power in baseball. Theo Epstein, a Beane disciple, became GM of the Boston Red Sox and in a few years turned them into World Champions, finally breaking the "Curse of the Bambino." (The Curse of the Bambino is the failure of Boston to win a championship since they traded Babe Ruth in 1920.)

....

"I made baseball as much fun as doing your taxes."
Bill James

....

Advanced Analytics to some extent is now part of every team's front office. The addition of high-tech cameras to every park now makes the abundance of data nearly overwhelming. When Russell Martin, a catcher for the Pittsburgh Pirates became a free agent, he found that his open market value had been raised considerably because he was the best catcher at framing pitches. Framing a pitch is catching it in such a way as to convince the umpire that it was in the strike zone, when perhaps it was not. Martin gave his pitchers many more strikes over the course of a season than a catcher who was less gifted at framing the pitch. Measuring this was possible with the additional technology of all those cameras. And that's just a small piece of what's now available. Want to know bat speed, exit velocity of the ball or defensive range of an infielder? No problem. Now the question is, "What do we do with all this information?"

Bill James even got hired by the Boston Red Sox as a consultant.

Football has been ahead of baseball for years when it comes to analysis. Twenty-two players moving on every play does not allow the naked eye to take it all in. Film and football have gone hand-in-hand almost from the beginning. Every player gets graded on every play. Videotape has made the physical process easier and computers have helped in analysis of tendencies of the other team and their own. The current controversy in football analytics revolves around whether teams punt too much. Most of the analytics guys feel that teams are too conservative when it comes to giving up the ball on fourth down. With decent field position and only a few yards for a first down, analytics guys say it is advisable to go for the first down rather than the traditional and conservative punt. What the analytics guys don't factor in is that any play outside the orthodox playbook that fails will be crucified in the press and on the radio for at least a week. Coaches whose jobs are even a little bit insecure may not be able to take the risk.

It's only a matter of time before a coach in a secure position is going to start listening to these guys and, if they are correct, will change the "conventional wisdom" of the game.

Unlike baseball, professional basketball embraced advanced analytics early on. So early, in fact, that not a whole lot of information regarding it was available to the general population. Teams quickly hired people who understood how to measure different aspects of a team sport that didn't have a lot of ways of measuring it, and kept that information to themselves.

The stats guys quickly decided that the best shot in basketball was the three-point attempt from the corner, as it was shorter than the other three-point shots, and of course worth 1.5 times a regular basket.

Cameras in all the arenas also led to other information. Ability to protect the basket was measurable, along with tendencies and success ratios of opposing players. Interesting things began to emerge, even if they were not publicized. Kyle Korver, one of the best three point shooters in the league, increased his team's offensive efficiency even when he didn't touch the ball. The threat of his making a three-point shot kept his defender from helping out on defense, and thus made

Korver's teammates more successful. That information had to be useful at contract negotiation time, yet totally unavailable in the past. Want to know how many feet Lebron James is running in a game? They have it. Does the fact that he's been covering less court in his last few games mean he's tired, no matter what he says? Possibly.

Teams that use this data may have an edge on teams that don't. The owner of the record-breaking Golden State Warriors implies that his team is light years ahead in this and other departments, and we thought it was Steph Curry and Co. dropping three-pointers from everywhere outside of San Francisco Bay who were winning all those games.

"Beware of Geeks bearing formulas."
Warren Buffett

Charles Barkley and Shaquile O'Neal like the analytics of their day, because they favor players like themselves. Scoring and rebounding are analytics, simple ones, but analytics none the less. Both were good scorers and good rebounders. Defensively they may not have measured up, and neither was a good three-point shooter, but nobody was really able to measure defense. Shaq was such a notoriously bad free throw shooter that other teams started the practice of "Hack-a-Shaq", just fouling him and hoping he wouldn't make very many free throws. How many games did this shortcoming cost his team? I'm sure he doesn't want to ask the analytics guys that question.

The question in sports is no longer "Are advanced analytics valuable?" The only remaining question is "How valuable are they?"

For every analytics disciple, there will be an "Old School" player who strongly suggests that "they really don't understand the game" and every time an analytics based team falters they will puff out their chests and proclaim how right they were.

The battle is ongoing, but the idea of better measuring players and strategies is not going away, despite the obstinacy of the "Old Guard." There's now just too much money involved.

More Basketball
Cousy and the Kids

More Basketball
Cousy and the Kids

*"Then one day, my mama bought me a basketball,
and I loved that basketball.*

*I took that basketball with me everywhere I went. That basketball
was like a basketball to me. I even put that basketball
underneath my pillow. Maybe that's why I can't sleep at night."*

From "Basketball Jones" by Cheech and Chong

The "Jones" referred to in "Basketball Jones" is a slang term for an addiction. Through the years there have been a few basketball players, athletic enough for the NBA, who have had a "Basketball Jones", for it takes no less than living with your basketball and dribbling day and night to achieve the ball handling skills that these men have achieved. It began with Bob Cousy. First, in college at Holy Cross and then with the Boston Celtics, Cousy was one of the first to go behind the back, through the legs and any other which way to beat a defender or complete a pass. Sleight of hand and deception were part and parcel of his offensive arsenal which propelled the Celtics deep into the playoffs year after year through the 1950s and into the 60s.

Unfortunately for Cousy, The NBA of that era was not a frequent visitor to any one of the three national TV networks, so his brilliance was rarely on display for those outside the Boston area.

The mid-60s brought us Pistol Pete Maravich at LSU. Coached by his father Press, whose coaching style took full advantage of Pete's extraordinary talents, Pete averaged over 40 points a game for three seasons at LSU while dazzling the Louisiana fans with his ball-handling wizardry. Like Steph Curry today, even Pete's pregame warmup drew crowds.

Maravich was to be the big draw for the New Orleans Jazz, the latest NBA expansion team. Pete was every bit the showman and star that the team and league needed, but NBA TV exposure was still slight and New Orleans wasn't in the playoffs when the network coverage would kick in. When he was finally with a good team, a knee injury had made him a shell of his former self.

The 1970s brought us Ernie Digregorio out of Providence. A Final Four appearance with Providence preceded being drafted by the Buffalo Braves of the ABA. His first year he led the league in Assists and Free Throw Percentage while entertaining the fans with a wide variety of dribbling and passing maneuvers that rivalled Pete Maravich.

Injuries shortened Ernie's career to the extent that he never reproduced those rookie numbers; he was out of the league after only five seasons.

The 1980s belonged to Earvin "Magic" Johnson of Michigan State and the Los Angeles Lakers. Magic was unusual for this group as he stood 6'9" tall, playing guard. Not the dribbler these others were, he used his height for great court vision and awareness and was the most exciting passer of his generation. With Magic leading the "Showtime" Lakers on the fast break, the ball might go anywhere but would soon surely go through the hoop.

The late 1990s brought us Steve Nash, consummate offensive player and ballhandler extraordinaire. Nash is one of the few members of the 50-40-90 club having shot 40% from three point range, 50% on his two point shots and 90% from the foul line. Larry Bird and Steph Curry also achieved this milestone. A two-time MVP with the Phoenix Suns, he was the perennial leader in assists while being entertaining as can be.

How entertaining? I think it is best summed up by an aristocratic, drama coach friend of mine who, when asked what sports he watched said, "I watch English Premier League Football and any game that Steve Nash is in."

Nash was a superb dribbler, passer and showman who, among other things, delighted in passing the ball through the legs of the defenders. Shortly after Nash, Jason Williams appeared, sounding as if he'd just crawled out of the Florida Everglades even though he originally hailed from West Virginia. Williams was nicknamed "White Chocolate" for his flair with the basketball. I think the only thing Jason could not do with a basketball was throw a two-handed chest pass to the person directly in his line of vision. Length-of-the-court bounce passes, behind-the-back passes, behind-the-back-sent-back-the-same-way-off-his-elbow passes and through-the-legs, over-the-shoulder and no-look passes were run of the mill for "White Chocolate." He was far and away the most entertaining playmaker since Maravich. For twelve years he delighted fans in Sacramento, Memphis, Miami and finally in Orlando.

This brings us to Steph Curry. The 7th pick of the Golden State Warriors in the 2009 NBA draft, Curry has led the league in three-pointers made the last four years, breaking the record in 2015 with 286 and shattering it the next with 402. He is an excellent passer with either hand and an extraordinary dribbler. His great footwork and dribbling allows him to get to the basket or free himself for an open three-pointer seemingly at will. He's only 6' 3" but in 886 three-point attempts this season has had only 1 (one!!!) blocked.

A unanimous winner of his second MVP award in 2016, he joins Steve Nash and Magic Johnson as the only point guards to win the award twice. As I mentioned earlier, his ball handling warmup drills, featuring two balls at once, are a must-see for Golden State fans.

What separates all these players from the pack is this: The first question you ask if you haven't seen their game is "What did XX do last night?" If you have seen the game, it's "Did you see what XX did last night?" After that you discuss who won and lost.

These guys entertain at an extremely high level; above and beyond winning and losing. They have an element of showmanship that seems to be innate, and if that's not who you are, no amount of coaching can create it.

So why don't we see more of it? Are these guys really game changers? I believe the answer to the second question is a resounding "No!" If they were game changers, we would see far more of them than we do. The answer to the first is a little more complicated.

The skill level required to accurately deliver passes from all angles or dribble in a way that makes a defender look just silly is ridiculously difficult to acquire. It does indeed take a "Basketball Jones." Hours and hours of practice for years and years. That's just the skill part. The showmanship comes from within.

Bob Cousy, the first of the great and flashy ball handlers, learned to use his left hand after he broke his right arm.

Pete Maravich's father loved him only through basketball. Pete was a troubled soul, but you'd never know it through the joy with which he played the game.

Steve Nash got his footwork from playing soccer. The drills that Steph Curry does that so captivate the fans were designed and used by Nash.

Jason Williams has highlight reels dotting Youtube from his high school days in West Virginia. Even then, the simple pass was almost unknown to him.

Steph Curry, son of NBA sharpshooter Dell Curry, was a great shooter in high school but most big colleges thought he was too small for the big time. Two outstanding NCAA Tournaments at Davidson proved them wrong. As his confidence grew, so did his ball handling until any pass was within his repertoire. This led to too many turnovers (a chronic problem for the great passers) until he became a little more discreet.

When you are lucky enough to be able to see one of these guys, do not squander the opportunity. You can't predict when one will appear, or how long he will be on the scene, and most importantly, when and if another one will ever show up.

Here's a thought to emphasize this point. Floating around is the idea that yesteryear's hyper kids, who could always be found dribbling a basketball, may now be "normalized" through the use of medications for ADD such as Ritalin. So you'd better take advantage of opportunities to see these guys, for those opportunities may soon vanish.

Spud Webb

"It's not the size of the man in the fight, but the size of the fight in the man."
Popular locker room saying

Every sport has players who do not look the part. Baseball has overweight pitchers and hitters who can still throw and hit. Tennis has players who are too small or too big to play the game properly. Basketball has guys who are just too small for a game that favors height.

Spud Webb at 5' 7" and 132 lbs led his high school basketball team in scoring (26ppg), led Midland Jr. College to the National Championship in 1983 – leading all scorers in the title game-and played two seasons at North Carolina State.

Drafted in the 4th Round and 87th overall in 1985 (they don't draft that many anymore) Spud played for the Atlanta Hawks for seven seasons and several teams thereafter.

He averaged 10 points and 5 assists over a 13 year career and won a slam dunk contest besides.

Before Spud, the only small guard in the NBA was Slater Martin, way back in the 1950s when the game was quite different, and Calvin Murphy in the 1970s.

The great Calvin Murphy (5' 9"), a 2nd round draft pick in 1970 who scored over 17,000 points in a 13-year career, should have been the trailblazer here, but it took over a decade for Spud Webb to arrive. Perhaps Murphy, who averaged over 30 ppg every year in college was perceived as a "fluke" rather than a type, making other teams reluctant to draft a look-alike.

Spud led the way for Muggsy Bogues (5' 3"), Nate Robinson (5' 9") and Earl Boykins (5' 5") to follow as super-short NBA players. Guys like J.J. Barea (5' 11") ten-year veteran and still going, and Isaiah Thomas(5' 9"), currently of the Boston Celtics and among the league leaders in scoring, are just the latest iteration of this phenomenon.

It's amazing how many undersized players overachieve their draft order and still the next small guy goes late in the draft or isn't drafted at all. I believe the league is now beginning to understand that the two key elements to success in the NBA are length, (these guys don't have that), and quickness, which these guys have in abundance. Still, they get overlooked.

Calvin Murphy is a Hall-of-Famer and a 2nd round pick. Spud Webb was 87th. Earl Boykins was undrafted and a 12 year veteran. J.J. Barea was undrafted. Muggsy Bogues is that rare 1st round pick (12th overall). He played 13 seasons, 10 with the Charlotte Hornets, leading the league twice in assists and is the career leader in Charlotte for minutes played, assists and steals. Nate Robinson is another 1st round pick (21st overall) who played ten years for a variety of teams. Isaiah Thomas was the last player drafted in 2011 at no. 60. None were drafted in the top ten, but all have played better than top ten picks from their draft year.

In my search through the drafts of the last fifteen years it is rare to find players under 6' drafted at all. Those that are drafted are usually over-achievers. As the NBA game has changed into a more widely spaced offense with three-point shooters stationed everywhere, quicker players are more valuable than ever.

Despite the success of these smaller players, I don't believe general managers know how to properly evaluate them and consequently avoid them. They don't come along that often, so there aren't a lot of other players to compare them to. Draft a 7-footer who doesn't work out and fans disapprove, but draft an undersized guard that fails and the fans, and possibly the owner, go nuts. That kind of reaction affects job security, and GMs are all about job security.

More Tennis

More Tennis

As I mentioned in the beginning, tennis is different from most sports in that it was an amateur sport for eighty years, and so, when players turned professional in 1968, they had a lot of catching up to do. No one was better suited to do just that than Billie Jean King. Fortunately, she had Chris Evert and Martina Navratilova to give her the drawing cards and rivalry that she needed. Nick Bolletieri came along to help keep the talent pool overflowing.

Billie Jean King

"Activism that challenges the status quo, that attacks deeply rooted problems, is not for the faint of heart."
Malcolm Gladwell

Billie Jean King is the Matriarch of women's professional tennis. Almost nothing has happened in the history of women's pro tennis that she has not been associated with.

She's won 129 singles titles, including 12 Grand Slam events. She won 20 titles in singles, doubles and mixed doubles just at Wimbledon. For 20 years she was a force to be reckoned with on the court.

Off the court, in 1970, along with Gladys Heldman, owner and editor of "World Tennis" magazine, she founded the women's pro tour under the sponsorship of Virginia Slims. Sure, it was odd that as late as the 1970s when cigarette advertising was banned from television, a cigarette company would be sponsoring the first women's tennis circuit, but beggars can't be choosers.

She was the first player to reach the $100,000 mark in a single year in 1971. Chris Evert earned $1,000,000 in career earnings in 1976, becoming the first female athlete to do so. It took just five years for that jump. Not bad.

The Virginia Slims Tour turned into the Women's Tennis Association (WTA) in 1973, expanding worldwide with a variety of sponsors in 1981.

In 1973, Billie Jean took part in "The Battle of the Sexes", the most watched tennis event in history with 30,000 live and an estimated 50 million on TV. King defeated 55 year-old self-proclaimed male chauvinist Bobby Riggs, 6-3, 6-3, 6-4. Riggs, a former Wimbledon champion had defeated Margaret Court on Mother's Day; King had to represent all of women's tennis.

She later said that she felt women's tennis would have been set back fifty years if she had lost. Given the stakes, few of King's contemporaries would have wanted anyone else defending their honor. Many described Billie Jean King as the greatest competitor they'd ever faced.

In 2006, The USTA National Tennis Center was renamed the USTA Billie Jean King National Tennis Center.

She has been in the center of every major movement for change in her lifetime. No matter if it was civil rights, gay rights or particularly women's rights, Billie Jean has been right there speaking out and taking the hits for all those to come, making their path a little easier. The male professionals began the "Association of Tennis Professionals" (ATP) in 1972, led by Donald Dell, Jack Kramer and Cliff Drysdale. Fighting for greater representation among the tournaments, bigger prize money and TV rights, the ATP has helped create modern professional tennis as it now stands. Billie Jean King and the WTA have fought for equal prize money at the majors and wherever men and women both play. Every step of the way the men probably had it easier than the women. Fortunately for the women, they had Billie Jean King.

Chris Evert

"Billie Jean King made us celebrities. Martina made us athletes."
Chris Evert

Chris Evert was the first teenage sensation of professional tennis. Raised on the clay courts of sunny south Florida and taught by her father Jimmy at the public park, she reached the semifinals of her very first pro tournament in 1969 at the tender age of 14. No one before or since has done as well in their first tournament.

Winner of 18 Grand Slam titles and 157 career wins, Evert is always listed among the best of all-time. Armed with ultra-consistent groundstrokes, a deceptive lob and drop shot, fierce concentration and an iron will, Evert reached the semifinals in 34 consecutive Grand Slam events. That is eight and a half years of incredible consistency. She was even better on clay, winning 125 matches in a row and seven French Open titles. Unlike the exuberant teens that would follow, Chris' intense focus and steely resolve earned her the nickname "The Ice Maiden." In England she was the "Ice Lolly."

How did she change the game of tennis? Every young player to come along after her looked like a tennis clone of Chris Evert. Everyone now had a two-handed backhand and they all looked like Evert's. Like Evert, they mostly avoided the net, relying on placement and consistency.

While they all looked like Evert, only Tracy Austin ever played like Evert. The brilliance of Chris Evert was in her precision and her cool demeanor. Others had consistency and beautiful two-handed backhands, but they lacked her overarching will to win and the tennis intelligence to make that happen.

The crowds were not particularly sympathetic to her until she became the underdog in her long historic rivalry with Martina Navratilova. A winner of 20 of 25 of their early matches, she won only 10 of the next 23, and then the upper hand went to Martina, when Martina transitioned from a chubby teenager into the fittest woman on the planet. The new Martina dominated Chris until Chris got fitter and stronger herself. No longer did practice consist of two hours hitting and that was it. Now it was off to the gym as well. The final tally was 43-37 for Martina.

At one point, from 1982-1987 they won 16 of 17 Grand Slam finals, with only Hana Mandlikova sneaking in a win in the 1985 U.S. Open.

The contrast in their games and personalities made for a truly enjoyable rivalry. Martina was forever aggressive, rushing the net at every opportunity. Chris was a counterpuncher, relying on precise placements and passing shots.

Martina wore her emotions on her sleeve; it was this emotional fragility that seemed to be the only hope that her opponents had. Evert was forever "The Ice Maiden", rarely showing any emotion at all.

Oddly, while everyone copied Chris Evert, particularly her backhand, almost no one fashioned their game after Martina. Actually, no one copied their game after champions Steffi Graf or Monica Seles either. It has been all Chris, all the time.

Martina Navratilova

*"The difference between involvement and commitment
is like the difference between ham and eggs.
The chicken is involved, the pig is committed.*

Martina

Martina Navratilova, born in Czechoslovakia and coached by her mother, made her professional tennis debut in 1973. Obviously talented, she made a dent in the tour almost immediately, making the French Open quarterfinals that same year.

She won her first title in 1974 and her first Grand Slam title in 1978 at Wimbledon, beating Chris Evert in the final. She won again in 1979 and held the year end #1 title.

While competitive with Evert, it wasn't until 1982 that she began to dominate Evert. A year earlier, she met Nancy Lieberman, the best female basketball player in college. With the women's professional basketball league folding, Nancy was looking for a new challenge.

Meanwhile, Renee' Richards, a fine senior men's player as Richard Raskind, had transitioned to a woman and was playing on the women's pro tour. She and Nancy, and later nutritionist Richard Haas, helped turn Martina into a fitter, tougher, more aggressive tennis player. This was her "team", and, while some of the participants changed, the "team" was always an integral part of her success.

Martina dominated the women's tour. In 1983 she compiled an 86-1 record, the best in the Open Era. You know she was fit when she started being compared to men.

To keep up, other players began spending more time in the gym as well as on the practice court, most notably Chris Evert. It was the only way they hoped to compete.

Martina won her last Grand Slam tournament in 1990 at Wimbledon at the age of 33. She lost the 1994 final at the age of 37.

She retired with 167 tournament wins and 18 Grand Slam titles and over a five-year period lost fewer than three matches a year.

As good as she was, she was not the player the younger players emulated. That was Chris Evert, although, beginning with Martina Hingis and continuing through to this day, many more young players are named Martina.

Besides leaving her mark on court, Martina has left her mark on today's game in the player's box in the stands. There sits the "team" of each competitor.

With the fantastic increase in prize and endorsement money for the top players, most have assembled a team to help them get to, or stay at, the top.

First and foremost is the coach. Sometimes there is more than one when a top player feels he needs someone who has been at the top before like Jimmy Connors, Boris Becker or Ivan Lendl, and someone who is there day to day. The rest of the team usually consists of a conditioning coach, a nutritionist, a hitting partner (particularly for the women), a psychologist and a massage therapist or trainer.

When these players win, the first thank-yous go to their "team".

And it's no longer just tennis. Golf has followed suit along with all other individual sports. Cost is the only limiting factor. Players in team sports are also expanding their support staff. The team provides many of these individuals, but many players prefer to have their own nutritionist, psychologist or trainer.

Tennis players who complained about playing Martina and her team soon adapted and got their own.

Unfortunately, this is a luxury that only the successful or rich can afford. The poor kid out playing the qualifiers for very little money is lucky if he has enough cash to get to the next tournament, let alone pay for an entourage. Sometimes the national association can assist young players in this regard, but if they are not on the radar as a potential top ten, forget about it. Until he can beat the guys with the entourage, he can't afford to get one of his own. It's not fair, but that's how it is.

Nick Bolletieri

"Don't let schooling interfere with your education."
Mark Twain

Sports in the 1950s, 60s and 70s were all pretty much the same. Play as a kid in Little league or PeeWee football or basketball and/or take a few tennis or golf lessons.

Most serious play began in high school with many of the better athletes starring in a different sport each season. A college scholarship was the reward at the end of the rainbow or possibly a Major League baseball contract.

The best of these might play in the pros for a few years before getting on with their life.

Nick Bolletieri was a man who came late to the game of tennis. He played one year in the 1950s for Spring Hill College in Alabama. Never heard of it? Neither have I.

After serving in the Army and dropping out of the University of Miami Law School Nick began teaching tennis. He worked at the Dorado Beach Hotel in Puerto Rico and then at The Colony Beach Resort and Hotel in Sarasota, Florida.

Nick had the idea that if you gave talented kids more time to practice and better competition to practice against, they could get a serious leg up on the competition.

At the Colony he gathered together 10 players who would attend a local private academy in the morning and hit tennis balls all afternoon. If he was right, his kids would start to make a dent in the junior rankings. He was right and they did.

In 1978, he saw Jimmy Arias and invited him to be part of his program. Jimmy led Nick's first group of kids and in 1980 he borrowed $1,000,000 and bought 40 acres of land near Bradenton, Florida. There he opened the Nick Bollettieri Tennis Academy, the first school of its kind.

In 1983 the Nick Bollettieri Tennis Academy ushered Jimmy Arias, 19 years old, to a victory in the Italian Open, semifinalist at the U.S. Open and the sixth ranked tennis player in the world.

Pros Carling Bassett and Kathy Horvath were also successful in '83 and the kids kept coming. There were enough parents willing to chase the dream and foot the bill, now $70,000+, for the academy. Yes, I said $70,000!

More success begat more success and the list of No. 1s who trained at Nick's place includes Andre Agassi, Jim Courier, Boris Becker, Monica Seles, Maria Sharapova and the Williams sisters among others.

At 82, Nick is still out on the court every day. He's a little less of a disciplinarian and a little more encouraging. In 2014 he was inducted into The International Tennis Hall of Fame. Always a promoter, he still manages to keep his Academy first on everyone's list, even if others are catching up.

His model was repeated in Florida and elsewhere, including throughout Europe. And not just for tennis.

In 1987 Nick sold out to Mark McCormack's International Management Group (IMG), who expanded to include golf, baseball, basketball, football, and soccer. It's still the Nick Bollettieri Tennis Academy and he's still there every day, but it's expanded to so much more.

Following the IMG model, high schools like Oak Hill Academy in Virginia and Findlay Prep in Arizona are basketball schools first, academic institutions a distant second. They play elite teams from around the country in front of college coaches and NBA scouts.

With the possible exception of football, elite high school athletes don't even think about playing for their high school team anymore.

And you thought talent was a "no strings attached" gift?

114

Sports and Society

Sports and Society

Sports has never existed in a vacuum. As much as fans may shout "Shut up and play ball, you're not getting paid to open your mouth," athletes live in the same world as you and I. Issues that affect us affect them as well, and they have a right to speak up if they so choose.

James Harris
FIRST BLACK NFL QUARTERBACK

"What a sad era when it is easier to smash an atom than a prejudice."
Albert Einstein

Yes, James Harris was the first black NFL quarterback to start in the NFL. Yes, Marlon Briscoe started one game for the Denver Broncos before Harris, but was really a wide receiver. Harris was 6'4" and 210 lbs, perfect size for a quarterback, but imperfect for most other positions, which is probably why he wasn't converted to wide receiver, defensive back, or running back as so many other black college quarterbacks had been.

He started four games for the Buffalo Bills in 1969 and began the 1970 season as the Bills' starting quarterback. He was traded to the Los Angeles Rams in 1973 and became the starting quarterback during the 1974 season, leading the Rams to wins in seven of their last nine games, a West Division title and victory in their first playoff game.

The fact that James Harris is in this book as a game changer is an embarrassment to me as an American. There is nothing particularly special about James Harris as a quarterback. He had a decent and perhaps above average career, and by all accounts was a decent human being, but certainly did not distinguish himself on the field in any lasting, meaningful way except that he was the first "black" quarterback.

Pro quarterback has always been a position of leadership and intelligence, two qualities that many sports fans of the day did not believe blacks possessed in abundance. It was just another barrier for African-Americans to overcome. Doug Williams is still mentioned as the first "black" quarterback to win a Super Bowl.

In researching this book I was amazed at how much race played a part in these black athletes' lives. The slights, indignities, and threats that they endured and overcame could fill up another book. I could have mentioned a few incidents for each of the black athletes in this book, but I have chosen to lump them all here and perhaps by sheer volume make a greater impression on the reader.

Everyone knows the death threats, hate-mail, taunts and name-calling that Jackie Robinson endured, but it did not end with him.

After leading the San Francisco Dons to two consecutive NCAA championships and a 56-game winning streak, Bill Russell was surprised he had not been named "The Best Big Man in the Northwest." That award went to a white ballplayer at another school.

Green Bay Packer great Paul Hornung didn't much care for trophies and kept his Heisman trophy in his garage. Did it have anything to do with winning it while quarterbacking Notre Dame to a 2-8 record, while the great Jim Brown was running wild at Syracuse en route to an 8-2 season?

In baseball, it became all too obvious that black athletes could compete with white athletes. Baseball statistics are cut and dried. Willie Mays, Hank Aaron, and others were posting superior numbers in homeruns, steals and batting average. Not even the most ardent racist could deny that they could compete. That's when the subtler form of racism began to creep in with claims that were much harder to verify or dispute. "Yes, they can hit homeruns but they can't hit in the clutch." "When the pressure is on, they wilt." Passed down from father to son, these unverifiable claims take a long time to disappear. On the 40th anniversary of Jackie Robinson's debut, Al Campanis, former General Manager of the Dodgers and a teammate of Robinson's, was asked why there weren't more black managers and general managers in baseball. Campanis famously replied "that blacks may not have some of the "necessities" to become a manager or a general manager." It is generally agreed that Campanis was a decent guy and fair to black ballplayers, and a man out of his element on national TV, but there it is, the unspoken thoughts of white America.

Early 1950s joke: How many black ballplayers on a major league roster? Two – one star and one to room with him on the road.

Just to clarify the above: Latin ballplayers could room with blacks, but not with whites. Latin ballplayers were not immune from the racism directed towards blacks.

Newspapers weren't innocent either. Roberto Clemente, star for the Pittsburgh Pirates, got tired of pitchers throwing at his head and stormed the mound demanding to pitch. Headline in the Pittsburgh Press the next day showed a picture of Clemente on the mound with the caption "Let mee peetch!!!" Really?! If stuttering Bob White had stormed the mound, the headline wouldn't have read "L-L-Let m-m--e p-p-p-pitch!"

The 1966 AFL All-Star Football Game was moved from New Orleans to Houston at the 11th hour when the players refused to play in New Orleans because of the terrible treatment of the black players by the entire city. Players could couldn't get a cab or find a restaurant which would seat them.

The 1958 University of Buffalo football team turned down a rare bowl invitation when the Tangerine Bowl committee in Orlando, Florida insisted that they not bring along their two black players.

Two time NBA league MVP Bill Russell was asked by a white fan on the retirement of Bob Cousy, "What are you gonna do, Russell, now that you don't have Cousy to carry you?" Russell politely reminded him who the league MVP was.

1960s Joke: How many blacks do you play on your basketball team? Two at home, three on the road, and five if you are down in the fourth quarter.

The 1960 World Series had one of the great endings of all time with Bill Mazeroski's homerun in the bottom of the ninth, winning the series for the Pirates and for the nine-year-old boy who would someday write this book. The only existing copy of this game is owned by a fan who set his camera up in front of his television and recorded the entire game and the post-game interviews.

In 1960 the Pirates had five black or Latin ballplayers including Joe Christopher, Gene Baker and star Roberto Clemente. During the raucous post-game celebration, team announcer Bob Prince called player after player up to the makeshift podium in the middle of the clubhouse. My unofficial count was that 17 players spoke. None of the black or Latin players appeared on television, including Clemente.

Roberto Clemente died December 31st, 1972 while still a Pittsburgh Pirate, attempting to deliver relief supplies to earthquake victims in Nicaragua when his plane crashed. There is now a statue of him in front of PNC Park, where the Pirates now play, but in 1960 they didn't want him seen on television.

There were positives throughout these times. Mississippi State won the Southeast Conference championhip in basketball in 1959, '61, and '62 and always turned down an invitation to play in the NCAA championship because of the integrated schools they would have to play. There were no Negroes playing in the Southeast Conference.

They won again in 1963, but 1963 was different. In the fall of 1962 James Meredith, a black man, accompanied by federal marshals, integrated the University of Mississippi. The Miss. St. president allowed the basketball team to go the NCAAs "unless hindered by competent authority."

A "competent authority" was soon found. A chancery court judge issued an injunction to keep the school from violating "the public policies of the state of Mississippi."

To avoid the injunction the coaches and players crept out of the state on a chartered plane and flew to East Lansing, Michigan to face the Ramblers of Loyola of Chicago. Loyola started four black players, unusual for the day, even in the North.

Loyola went on to win the game 61-51 on their way to winning the NCAA tournament. The Mississippi State players, whose only desire was to compete against the best, did not encounter the backlash they feared upon their return home.

There were white segregationist Mississippians who feared the issue was "the greatest challenge to our way of life since Reconstruction" and a threat to "our southern way of life," but soon the Southeast Conference was integrated and life moved on.

In 2016 in my new hometown of Buffalo, NY I had lunch with a group of friends when an acquaintance of theirs joined us and announced that he was rooting against the Carolina Panthers in the 2016 Super Bowl because of the N-----r they had at quarterback. Apparently Cam Newton didn't conform to his view of what a good African-American should be. I guess we haven't changed as much as we would like to think.

Makes me proud to be an American!

Muhammad Ali

"Man, I ain't got no quarrel with them Viet Cong. Why should they ask me to put on a uniform and go ten thousand miles from home and drop bombs and bullets on brown people in Vietnam while so-called Negro people in Louisville are treated like dogs and denied simple human rights?"
Muhammad Ali

Despite the platform that celebrity provided, very few athletes ever spoke out about the controversial issues of their day. Most players were not rich enough to jeopardize their paychecks by speaking out against injustice.

Muhammad Ali may have been the best boxer of the 20th Century. From 1960, when he won the Olympic Gold Medal, to 1964 when he defeated Sonny Liston for the heavyweight title, no heavyweight had ever moved like him and very few had ever boxed like him.

Undefeated and outspoken, he forced every boxing fan, and most everyone else, to take notice when he joined the Nation of Islam and changed his name from Cassius Clay to Muhammad Ali. Many refused to call him by his new name, insisting on calling him Cassius Clay, what Ali now referred to as his "slave" name.

Ali was drafted by the U.S. Army in April, 1967 and refused induction. Arrested for failure to report, he was convicted in June of 1967, his conscientious objector status being denied, a verdict which was upheld by the Court of Appeals. At this time he was also stripped of his boxing license. The Supreme Court overruled his conviction in June of 1971, citing that no reason was given for denying his conscientious objector status.

As resistance to the Vietnam War grew and the Civil Rights movement was expanding, Muhammad Ali became a popular speaker on college campuses. Unable to box for almost four years, Ali stood as a symbol of resistance against the war and against racial injustice. He was revered in the black community for standing up for his rights.

Whenever an athlete in this time period, white or black, did speak out on social issues, he often heard "You get paid to hit/shoot/run, not talk" as if being a professional athlete made you less of a citizen. Many athletes stood by Ali, notably Cleveland Browns star Jim Brown and Boston Celtics center Bill Russell, but most were silent.

Once again able to fight, he began his comeback against undefeated current champion Joe Frazier in Madison Square Garden in the most-watched fight in history. Three and one-half years out of boxing were too much for Ali to overcome against a man whose style and courage were always hard for him to defeat. He lost a fifteen round decision.

After a series of victories and one loss to Ken Norton when his jaw was broken, he defeated Joe Frazier in January of 1974 and regained the heavyweight title, defeating George Foreman in the "Rumble in the Jungle" in Zaire in October 1974.

He fought into 1981 for a total of 61 professional fights and record of 56-5, retiring at the age of 38.

....

""Impossible is just a big word thrown around by small men who find it easier to live in the world they've been given than to explore the power they have to change it. Impossible is not a fact. It's an opinion. Impossible is not a declaration. It's a dare. Impossible is potential. Impossible is temporary. Impossible is nothing."

Muhammad Ali

....

In 1984 he was diagnosed with Parkinson's Disease, a neurological ailment highlighted by uncontrollable tremors. Tragically, Ali, one of the most interesting speakers in history, became limited in his speech, severely so in his later years.

He died in 2016 at the age of 74.

The Rev. Al Sharpton may have described him best when he said

"For the heavyweight champion of the world, who had achieved the highest level of athletic celebrity, to put all of that on the line – the money, the ability to get endorsements – to sacrifice all of that for a cause, gave a whole sense of legitimacy to the movement and the causes with young people that nothing else could have done. Even those who were assassinated, certainly lost their lives, but they didn't voluntarily do that. He knew he was going to jail and did it anyway. That's another level of leadership and sacrifice."

Coming Out

There have always been gay athletes. The ancient Greeks celebrated it, at least among men. Modern America, Christian America, Protestant and Catholic America, not so much! Women, of course, didn't matter much. Athletes who were gay have kept their sexuality a secret until very recently.

First, let's divide them up into three groups: women, men in macho sports, and men in less masculine sports.

Women: It used to be that girls who gravitated to sports over dolls and dresses were described as tomboys, and while it was cute for awhile, eventually they were going to have to learn how to be wives, homemakers, and mothers. Those who rebelled from this path were thought to be unusual at best, dikes and lesbians at worst. This was a problem for sports like tennis and golf, which women, sometimes lesbian women, could play quite well and entertainingly, but didn't want to turn off their potential audience.

Macho men: sports like baseball, football, basketball and hockey were way too macho to allow any hint of homosexuality to be allowed to enter the locker room. The gay athletes among them either seemed to share in the womanizing ways of their peers or were seen as private, quiet and introspective. Coming out was not an option.

Men in less masculine sports: less masculine sports included figure skating, diving, and to a lesser extent, tennis and golf, which were country club sports and so by definition were not as masculine as the sports played by the hard-working laborers of this country. The fact that a male figure skater might be gay would be less shocking, but not something that would be admitted; at least not for a long time.

So when did it change and who changed it? Like most change in America, it was not one thing but many, and over a fairly long period of time.

Perhaps it began with the Stonewall riots in New York City in 1969, when gay men rebelled against the constant harassment by the NYPD for offenses against the law which did no harm. This was the unofficial start of the gay rights movement.

A chronology follows of important events in the history of gay participation in pro sports in America.

1975-77: Dave Kopay, nine year running back for the New Orleans Saints, announces in '75 that he's gay and publishes his book "The Dave Kopay Story" in '77. He's the first player from a major sport to admit to being gay. In the next 40 years only four other football players come out of the closet and all after their careers are over: Roy Simmons in 1992, Esera Tuaolo in 2002, Wade Davis in 2012, and Kwame Harris in 2013. All talk about how hard it was to focus on football and keep their sex lives secret at the same time.

1988: Greg Louganis, after sweeping the diving gold medals in both the 1984 and 1988 Olympics, announces that he is gay and HIV positive. Louganis goes on to a healthy career as an activist, actor and diving coach.

Brian Boitano won the 1988 gold in men's figure skating, but doesn't officially come out until 2013, shortly before the Sochi Olympics in Russia, in opposition to Vladimir Putin's crackdown on gays.

American figure skating champion Johnny Weir also announces he is gay.

Meanwhile, on the women's side, in tennis, both Billie Jean King and Martina Navratilova, in 1981 admitted their relationship with women: Martina in a book, and Billie Jean King in a palimony lawsuit. BJK said she lost all her endorsements almost immediately.

Two time Grand Slam winner Amelie Mauresmo came out when she was 19, in 1998, and attributed her improved play to the fact that she no longer had to worry about hiding her sexuality. Subsequently, other women players have come out during their careers with no major negative consequences.

On the men's side, as I said earlier, tennis as a country club sport was always a little suspect in the public's eye and the scandal involving young men surrounding former champion Bill Tilden in the early 1950s didn't help. Former player Ted Tinling, who was openly gay, was the chief dress designer for the women on tour. It would not have been particularly surprising if a male player or two had come out as gay since, but no male player has. I do not care to speculate on why this is.

U.S. World Cup and Olympic soccer star Abby Wambach, who married her longtime partner in 2013, and teammate Megan Rapinoe, who came out in 2012, have suffered no ill effects regarding endorsements or teammates.

Britney Griner and Sheryl Swoopes are WNBA stars who came out.

John Amaechi, an Englishman, played eight years in various pro basketball leagues including the NBA, retiring in 2003. He came out in 2007 with the publication of his book "Man in the Middle", becoming the first former NBA player to admit to being gay.

Billy Bean (not to be confused with former major leaguer and general manager for the Oakland A's), a major leaguer for six seasons, retired in 1995 and came out in 1999. He is currently Major League Baseball's first "Ambassador for Inclusion."

As I said in the beginning, it has always been assumed that some of the women athletes were gay and that some of the men in sports like diving or figure skating might be gay. All these admissions, with the exception of the football players, one basketball player, and one baseball player, do not upset America's view of masculinity and sports, particularly when the players announce their sexuality only after their retirement.

Who does change our view on this subject are our next two game changers.

Jason Collins

"I didn't set out to be the first openly gay athlete playing in a major American team sport. But since I am, I'm happy to start the conversation."
Jason Collins

As a 6'10 1/2'" journeyman center in the NBA, Stanford educated and an identical twin, Jason Collins is used to having no place to hide. At the end of the 2012-2013 Jason decided to come all the way out of hiding and in a May 2013 article became the first active major team-sport player to announce that he was gay.

There was no major backlash amongst his fellow NBA players, many of whom openly supported him, or by sports fans in general, and while Collins didn't get back in uniform until 2014 with the New Jersey Nets, there also was no organizational backlash. Of course there were one or two players and talking heads who couldn't help showing their intolerance of Collins. They were the ones who suffered the backlash. Collins' jersey, #98 in honor of Matthew Shepard, a gay young man killed in a horrific hate crime, was one of the hottest-selling properties among all NBA merchandise.

Always a tough, physical defender, Collins held his own with the biggest centers in the league. He finished the 2014 season with the Nets and promptly announced his retirement from pro basketball.

"Time" magazine named him one of the "**world's most influential people for 2014.**"

Michael Sam

Michael Sam was a defensive end at the University of Missouri, the Southeast Conference Defensive Player Of The Year for 2013, and a unanimous All-America selection. In August of 2013 he informed his teammates that he was gay, and he asked that that information remain with the team.

His teammates were supportive and no mention was made of his sexuality during the 2013 season. In an "Outside the Lines" segment on ESPN in February of 2014 Sam announced his sexuality.

Sam was initially projected as a 3rd or 4th round draft selection in the upcoming 2014 NFL Draft. After his announcement, some NFL executives anonymously speculated that his draft status could drop with his announcement.

He was eventually drafted in the 7th round by the St. Louis Rams, 249th out of 256 players drafted. He stayed on the Rams' roster until the final cut to 53 players. The Dallas Cowboys signed him for their practice squad, but released him six weeks later.

He briefly played for the Montreal Alouettes of the Canadian Football League, but never really committed to playing in the CFL.

He is currently out of football.

Both Collins and Sam have made it easier for the next player in a major team sport to announce that he is gay, although I'm sure many will still be reluctant to do so. As I said, most change in America comes gradually.

We haven't even begun to talk about Renee Richards and transsexuals in sports. While Richards, as a 41-year-old man turned woman was good enough to play on the women's pro tour, she was not good enough, or, more importantly, young enough to dominate. A court decided that the WTA could not require a genetic test to determine if Richards could play, which was a big victory for transgender rights. She eventually achieved a ranking of #20 in singles without ever winning a tournament.

And if that doesn't complicate things enough, how about Caster Semenya, the South African middle distance runner subjected to controversial gender testing over claims that she was using performance enhancing drugs, or actually was producing testosterone in quantities similar to a man. Her victory in the 2016 Olympics in the 800 meters, while a personal triumph and a cause for celebration in South Africa, is seen by many as a win for someone with an unfair advantage.

David Epstein writes in his book "The Sports Gene", a book on genetic advantages, that one of the prevailing theories in the 1970s was that women were catching up to men in all the measurable sports: running, weightlifting, jumping, and it was only a matter of time before they were equal to the men. The theory was that only recently had women begun to train like men, and this was the reason for their rapid improvement. It turned out that their performance acceleration was not due to training like men, but mostly due to testosterone injections. They weren't catching up to the men, they were just becoming more like the men.

Estrogen, testosterone and sports are going to be linked for a long time.

Patsy Mink and Edith Green

"If a woman wants publicity, she should have quintuplets."
Bobby Riggs

"I just had to play. Title IX had just passed, and I wanted to change the hearts and minds of people to match the legislation."
Billie Jean King in an interview after defeating Bobby Riggs in
"The Battle of the Sexes" tennis match

In 1969 I played high school sports with a future NFL linebacker, who also excelled in baseball and basketball. His girlfriend could outrun him at any distance, any day of the week. She was a cheerleader. What a waste. (This is no knock on modern cheerleaders, who now display just as much athleticism as the boys.)

Patsy Mink, a third generation Japanese-American was the first non-white, Asian American to serve in Congress. Edith Green, who led the passage of the Equal Pay Act, was considered the most powerful woman to ever serve in congress.

Together with Senator Birch Bayh (D-IN), they are responsible for passing the "Title IX Amendment of the Higher Education Act" in 1972, prohibiting discrimination against women in all higher education programs receiving federal funding.

Generally referred to as "Title IX," this statute has had its most profound impact in sports. In 1972 7% (300,000) of high school girls participated in sports. Today that number is 41% (3,000,000).

In 1972, 2% of athletic budgets went to girls programs. They were often limited to cheerleading and, surprisingly, square dancing.

Female programs were discriminated against in other ways. Scholarships, equipment, uniforms, travel budgets, practice schedules, and coaching salaries were often inferior to the men's programs.

Thanks to Title IX, by 1976 much of that had changed, but not without plenty of resistance. Over twenty lawsuits have been filed challenging all or parts of the statute.

In 1984, in Grove City v. Bell, the court ruled that only those programs directly receiving federal funds could be affected by the statute. Since very little federal funding goes directly to any specific program, this effectively neutralized the law.

Congress rewrote the law in 1988 to correct this and passed it over President Reagan's veto.

While most sports are played by men and women, the most significant one that is not, is football. Not only do girls not play football, lots and lots of boys do. This can make anything close to equal participation in sports difficult.

If sixty boys play high school football and they play most of the other sports that girls play, how do we make this equal? Equal opportunity may not make for equal outcomes.

At the Division I college level, football players receive the lion's share of scholarships. Creating an equal number of female scholarships makes for some interesting outcomes, which many find unfair.

For instance, the women's tennis team may have eight scholarships available while the men's team has two. Girls' softball or volleyball may have twice as many available scholarships as baseball or men's volleyball. Unfortunately, some schools have decided to drop certain men's sports to keep things equal. Men's tennis, wrestling, golf and other sports may be cut even though they are successful and relatively inexpensive. This is equality by subtraction, not something the law was intended to do.

An argument that has been rejected in many forms is that girls have less interest in playing sports than boys. This was one of the original arguments against Title IX. What they found was that "If you build it, they will come." Participation exploded to the point where high school girls play at nearly five times the number as did prior to the passage of the law.

The benefits of women's participation in sports are many. Obesity is down. Smoking decreases. Teen pregnancy is lessened, and fewer girls drop out of school.

One of the original motivations for the law was the discovery that there were programs to keep boys from dropping out of school, but not girls. These were the times we lived in.

Girls now make up 52% of college students and receive 48% of athletic scholarships. In 1982, the first NCAA women's basketball champion-ships were held with Louisiana Tech defeating Cheney State. Cheney State coach, future Hall of Famer Vivian Stringer, tells of driving a broken down prison bus early in the program, prior to 1972. By 1982 Title IX had surely helped with the transportation.

One surprising change has to do with coaches. In 1972 90% of women's teams were coached by women. Today that number is 40%. Another "unintended" consequence!

Lance Armstrong

"We are what we pretend to be,
so we must be careful what we pretend to be."
Kurt Vonnegut

Quick quiz: Name two winners of the Tour de France. Answer: Lance Armstrong, and I can't think of another one. OK, some of you sports geeks can name five time winner Miguel Indurain or three time winner American Greg LeMond, but most of us can't. Until Lance Armstrong came along, no one gave a s---- about cycling and the Tour de France. When Lance began winning, we began to care.

And why wouldn't we? He had the perfect story. And the perfect name – Lance Armstrong. How perfect is that? Americans love a great story about overcoming adversity to reach the pinnacle of your sport.

Lance was diagnosed with advanced testicular cancer in October 1996 and given a very gloomy chance of survival. Several rounds of new chemotherapy drugs remarkably made him cancer-free. Before his cancer diagnosis, Armstrong had won four stages of the Tour de France, but never the whole Tour. With a clean bill of health, he was able to train again and returned for the 1999 Tour.

Having lost his previous sponsorship, he was offered a spot on the U.S. Postal Team. C'mon, it doesn't get any more apple pie American than the U.S. Post Office.

Armstrong won the 1999 Tour de France and America took notice. He won again in 2000 and for the next five years. At the end of the 2005 tour he retired from professional cycling.

From 1997, through his Lance Armstrong Foundation, he raised millions and millions for cancer research by selling his "Livestrong" bracelets. He was profiled everywhere and was one of America's most admired people, not just athletes. His endorsements through Nike and other companies brought him personal wealth as well.

> *"Extraordinary allegations require extraordinary evidence."*
> Lance Armstrong

Throughout his Tour de France triumphs there were hints and allegations that Armstrong had tested positive for illegal drugs, or that he was definitely using illegal drugs. Armstrong maintained that he had never tested positive for illegal substances and Americans, based on our long-held belief that we are innocent until proven guilty, chose to believe him. Besides, by this time, his story and celebrity were so woven into the American fabric that no one really wanted to take him down.

But down he went. Former teammate Floyd Landis, denied the 2006 Tour win when he tested positive, in 2010 revealed all the secrets of Lance and his teammates. A federal investigation followed, and despite years of denying any illegal drug activity, Lance admitted doping in an interview with Oprah Winfrey in 2013.

The U. S. Anti-Doping Agency named him as the ringleader of "the most sophisticated, professionalized and successful doping program that sport has ever seen."

Sponsors dropped him and lawsuits to recover payments and bonuses paid for winning the Tour de France popped up all over the place. He severed ties to the Livestrong Foundation to keep that organization from going bankrupt.

The real question is "Why did we ever believe him?" Coming back from toxic chemotherapy is hard enough. Coming back to world #1 status in a grueling aerobic sport like cycling has to stretch anyone's credulity. To top it all off, Armstrong was beating all the other cyclists who were caught doping. We know from Ben Johnson and others that that is a very hard thing to do. But believe him we did. Americans love a good comeback. As CNN put it –"The epic downfall of cycling's star, once an idolized icon of millions around the globe, stands out in the history of professional sports."

Americans didn't care about cycling before Lance Armstrong. Now they really, really don't care about it after having been burned by Lance Armstrong. We may never care again, no matter how good a story the next great American cyclist is.

Outliers

"Prediction is a difficult art. Especially when it involves the future."
Yogi Berra

We have arrived at the end without mentioning some people you probably thought had to be included in the book. If you had asked me, "Are they going to revolutionize the sport?" I would have said yes. I would have been wrong.

Venus and Serena Williams stormed onto the pro tennis scene achieving things no siblings had ever achieved. They were ranked #1 and #2 at the same time and played in Grand Slam finals against each other in 3 of the four majors. Serena is the all-time Grand Slam leader. Surely, little black girls would notice and there would be imitators.

They may have noticed, but there have been very few imitators. Sloan Stephens is about the only one, although there is a Japanese player with a black parent who looks and plays a lot like Serena Williams. Se ri Pak they are not.

Tiger Woods, the greatest celebrity in golf history, has a very diverse ethnic background. He was going to lead a surge in minority golf participation and hopefully a more diverse leader board. It didn't happen. After his sensationalized fall from grace, it's not going to happen. Se ri Pak he is not.

Wayne Gretzky, hockey's all-time leading scorer was going to lead the NHL to the promised land of equality with the other major sports. For too long hockey was soccer on ice, with scores of 2-1 or 1-0. Gretzky and the Edmonton Oilers changed all that and for a time hockey was scoring more than baseball.

Alas, they couldn't keep it up. While baseball was hitting homeruns out of the park with juiced up athletes, hockey was returning to its clutch and grab and keep the good players from playing good, but don't worry, there's a fight coming up soon. Every time a rule change comes along to open up the game, the conservative powers that be find a way to shut it down.

As great as Gretzky was, it's all a distant memory.

Every two years or so, America's feel good story is the **USA women's soccer team**. Whether it's the World Cup or the Olympics, you can count on the American women to compete for the Gold and for a women's professional soccer league to follow shortly thereafter. Unfortunately, before the next major world soccer event, the U.S. women's league has gone bankrupt.

Yes, thanks to Title IX and the very talented women on the Olympic team, thousands of girls play soccer. That fact cannot create a large enough fan base to sustain a pro league.

Rafael Nadal won nine consecutive French Open titles and is the undisputed greatest clay court player of all time. He achieved this greatness in large part to a forehand that imparted significantly more topspin on the ball than his competitors. Angled shots which were near impossible for his opponents were regular fare for Rafa.

Greats like Roger Federer were imparting up to 4600 rpms on their forehands while Nadal was at 5900 rpms. Not only did this allow him to keep more of his shots in the court and create better angles for those shots, but the extra spin on the ball made it explode off the court into his opponent. Fourteen Grand Slam titles and still going, the next generation of players will have lots of Nadal imitators. Nope, nada, uh-uh. No one in eleven years has copied the Nadal forehand. Maybe no one ever will.

It's hard to predict who will have the greatest impact on future generations.

Modern Sports: Pro and Con

Pros	Cons
More live sports on TV	*Major events on cable versus network*
Young players have a chance to become the best they can be	*Kids specialize too early, don't play HS sports, too much pressure early*
Players make a fair share of sports revenues gain	*17 Major labor stoppages to fair share*
Player agents help to get fair salaries and other endorsements	*Player holdouts turn off fans*
Modern medicine shortens time off due to injuries and lengthens careers	*Outstanding performances lead to suspicion of drug use*
Games are safer and less violent	*More aware of long term health risks*
More statistics for stats geeks	*Too many geeky stats*
Less racism today	*Today's racism stands out more*
More girls and women in sports than ever before	*Nothing wrong with that*
Sports keep kids active and healthy	*Sports too competitive. Too many kids dropping out younger and younger*

Epilogue

Looking ahead from 1951, no one could have envisioned what sports would look like in 2017. A look at Sports Illustrated through that year highlights some of the changes.

Baseball dominated from Spring training through the World Series, although it ended almost a month earlier. College and NFL football were equally covered, but only from September through November, plus Bowl Games. Basketball received about as much attention as golf and tennis, which is to say far less than now. Boxing and horseracing were more prominent and there were occasionally articles on chess and bridge, but they have all been replaced by NASCAR and various forms of Mixed Martial Arts (MMA).

That's one change. The athletes who play them is another. What would a football player from 1951 say when he saw a modern NFL offensive line? Or a typical NBA lineup? Bigger, stronger, faster has been the name of the game for a long time now.

As for the games themselves? The modern athlete, with superior nutrition, training, and practice performs at such a high level there might be question marks as to what planet these players are from.

Women's sports have come even farther. The entertainment quality of women's performances in sports like tennis, skating and gymnastics is equal to or superior to the men.

What does the future hold? I certainly don't know. More of the same? Doubtful. Robotic parts? Maybe. More commercials? Yes, more commercials. The fans will demand it.

I think I got that last one right, so I'll quit right here.

As I said in the introduction, this was not intended to be the ultimate word on modern sports. More like a starting point. I hope you liked it.

Acknowledgements

It is rare when a book can be written by the author alone. This is not one of those times. I need a lot of help and I got it. Mary Jo O'Connor edited the big picture while Jeff Jones, hereafter known as the comma king, focused on the small stuff. She hurt my feelings pointing out my poor writing while he was just annoying.

The look of the book can be credited to Joe Galanti while the cover design belongs to Mike Gelen. I'm barely able to type let alone design. Bev Kirby's moral support is always more important than she knows. Of course, my wife Joanne's understanding is always critical. When she asks "What are you doing today? and I reply that "I'm writing." and she doesn't put a shovel in my hand is how this book got written.

Thanks to you all.

www.ingramcontent.com/pod-product-compliance
Lightning Source LLC
Chambersburg PA
CBHW071003040426

42443CB00007B/642